W9-ATB-845

Coaching Youth Volleyball

Third Edition

American Sport Education Program

Human Kinetics

Library of Congress Cataloging-in-Publication Data

Coaching youth volleyball / American Sport Education Program.--3rd ed.
p. cm.
ISBN 0-7360-3796-9
1. Volleyball for children--Coaching. 2. Volleyball--Coaching. I. American Sport Education Program.
GV1015.5.C63 2001
796.325--dc21 2001016657

ISBN: 0-7360-3796-9

Copyright © 2001, 1997, 1993 by Human Kinetics Publishers, Inc.

All rights reserved. Except for use in a review, the reproduction or utilization of this work in any form or by any electronic, mechanical, or other means, now known or hereafter invented, including xerography, photocopying, and recording, and in any information storage and retrieval system, is forbidden without the written permission of the publisher.

Materials in chapter 4 are reprinted with permission from the YMCA of the USA, 1999, *YMCA Coaching Winners Baseball and Softball*. (Champaign, IL: Human Kinetics).

Acquisitions Editor: Russell Medbery, PhD; **Games Consultant**: Penny Moisson; **Managing Editor**: Wendy McLaughlin; **Assistant Editor**: Dan Brachtesende; **Copyeditor**: Jan Feeney; **Proofreader**: Susan Hagan; **Graphic Designer**: Fred Starbird; **Graphic Artist**: Sandra Meier; **Photo Manager**: Gayle Garrison; **Cover Designer**: Jack W. Davis; **Photographer (cover)**: Tom Roberts; **Photographer (interior)**: Tom Roberts, photos appearing on pages 1, 39, and 149 © Mary Langenfeld; **Art Manager**: Craig Newsom; **Illustrators**: Tom Janowski and Roberto Sabas; **Printer**: United Graphics

Copies of this book are available at special discounts for bulk purchase for sales promotions, premiums, fund-raising, or educational use. Special editions or book excerpts can also be created to specifications. For details, contact the Special Sales Manager at Human Kinetics.

Printed in the United States of America 10 9 8 7 6 5 4 3 2

Human Kinetics
Web site: www.HumanKinetics.com

United States: Human Kinetics, P.O. Box 5076, Champaign, IL 61825-5076
800-747-4457
e-mail: humank@hkusa.com

Canada: Human Kinetics, 475 Devonshire Road, Unit 100, Windsor, ON N8Y 2L5
800-465-7301 (in Canada only)
e-mail: orders@hkcanada.com

Europe: Human Kinetics, 107 Bradford Road, Stanningley
Leeds LS28 6AT, United Kingdom
+44 (0) 113 255 5665
e-mail: hk@hkeurope.com

Australia: Human Kinetics, 57A Price Avenue, Lower Mitcham, South Australia 5062
08 8277 1555
e-mail: liahka@senet.com.au

New Zealand: Human Kinetics, P.O. Box 105-231, Auckland Central
09-523-3462
e-mail: hkp@ihug.co.nz

Coaching Youth Volleyball

Contents

Welcome to Coaching! vii
Key to Diagrams viii

Chapter 1 **Stepping Into Coaching** 1

How to meet your responsibilities as a coach, how to coach when your child is on your team, and how to apply the five tools of an effective coach.

Chapter 2 **Communicating As a Coach** 9

How to send effective verbal and nonverbal messages to communicate better with players, parents, fans, officials, and opposing coaches.

Chapter 3 **Providing for Players' Safety** 17

How to provide for safety and respond to players' injuries when they do occur.

Chapter 4 **The Games Approach to Coaching Volleyball** 33

How to use the most effective method for teaching tactics and skills.

Chapter 5 **Teaching and Shaping Skills** 39

Learn the four steps of teaching skills effectively and how to shape skills, correct errors, and deal with misbehavior.

Chapter 6 **Game-Day Coaching** 53

How to prepare for the game, coach during the game, and keep winning and losing in perspective.

Chapter 7 **Rules and Equipment** 65

Understand rules, court size and markings, player equipment, game procedures, positions, and officiating signals.

Chapter 8 **Tactics and Skills** 81

Know the team tactics and individual offensive and defensive skills to teach to your players.

Chapter 9 **Season Plans** 149

Organize your practices throughout the season with sample plans for players 8 to 9, 10 to 11, and 12 to 14.

Appendix A Injury Report 161
Appendix B Emergency Information Card 163
Appendix C Emergency Response Card 165

Welcome to Coaching!

Coaching young people is an exciting way to be involved in sport. But it isn't easy. Some coaches are overwhelmed by the responsibilities involved in helping athletes through their early sport experiences. And that's not surprising, because coaching youngsters requires more than bringing the balls to the court and letting them play. It involves preparing them physically and mentally to compete effectively, fairly, and safely in their sport and providing them with a positive role model.

This book will help you meet the challenges *and* experience the many rewards of coaching young athletes. In this book you'll learn how to meet your responsibilities as a coach, communicate well and provide for safety, use a highly effective method—the games approach—to teaching tactics and skills, and learn strategies for coaching on game day. We also provide three sets of season plans to guide you throughout your season.

This book serves as a text for ASEP's Coaching Youth Sport course. If you would like more information about this course or other ASEP courses and resources, please contact us at

ASEP
P.O. Box 5076
Champaign, IL 61825-5076
1-800-747-5698

www.asep.com

Key to Diagrams

SR	=	Server
P	=	Player
H	=	Hitter
S	=	Setter
RF	=	Right front player
LF	=	Left front player
MF	=	Middle front player
RB	=	Right back player
LB	=	Left back player
MB	=	Middle back player

chapter 1

Stepping Into Coaching

If you are like most youth league coaches, you have probably been recruited from the ranks of concerned parents, sport enthusiasts, or community volunteers. Like many rookie and veteran coaches, you probably have had little formal instruction on how to coach. But when the call went out for coaches to assist with the local youth volleyball program, you answered because you like children and enjoy volleyball, and perhaps because you wanted to be involved in a worthwhile community activity.

Your initial coaching assignment may be difficult. Like many volunteers, you may not know everything there is to know about volleyball or about how to work with children. *Coaching Youth Volleyball* will help you learn the basics of coaching volleyball effectively.

To start, let's take a look at what's involved in being a coach. What are your responsibilities? We'll also talk about how to handle the situation when your child is on the team you coach, and we'll examine five tools for being an effective coach.

Your Responsibilities as a Coach

As a volleyball coach, you'll be called upon to do the following:

1. **Provide a safe physical environment.** Playing volleyball holds an inherent risk, but as a coach you're responsible for regularly inspecting the practice and competition courts (see the checklist for facilities and equipment in chapter 6).

2. **Communicate in a positive way.** You'll communicate not only with your players but also with parents, officials, and administrators. Communicate in a way that is positive and that demonstrates you have the best interests of the players at heart. Chapter 2 will help you communicate effectively and positively.

3. **Teach the tactics and skills of volleyball.** We'll show you an innovative "games approach" to teaching and practicing the tactics and skills young athletes need to know—an approach that kids thoroughly enjoy. We ask you to help all players be the best they can be. In chapter 5 we'll show you how to teach volleyball skills, and in chapter 9 we'll provide season plans for 8- to 9-year-olds, 10- to 11-year-olds, and 12- to 14-year-olds. In chapter 8 we'll provide descriptions of all the skills you'll need to teach and to help you detect and correct errors that players typically make.

4. **Teach the rules of volleyball.** We'll ask you to teach your players the rules of volleyball. You'll find the rules in chapter 7.

5. **Direct players in competition.** This includes determining starting lineups and a substitution plan, relating appropriately to officials and to opposing coaches and players, and making tactical decisions during games (see chapter 6). Remember that the focus is not on winning at all costs, but on coaching your kids to compete well, do their best, and strive to win within the rules.

6. **Help your players become fit and value fitness for a lifetime.** We want you to help your players be fit so they can play volleyball safely and successfully. We also want your players to learn to become fit on their own, understand the value of fitness, and enjoy training. Thus, we ask you not to make them do push-ups or run laps for punishment.

Make it fun to get fit for volleyball, and make it fun to play volleyball so they'll stay fit for a lifetime.

7. Help young people develop character. Character development includes learning caring, honesty, respect, and responsibility. These intangible qualities are no less important to teach than the skill of serving the ball well. We ask you to teach these values to players both by conducting Team Circles after every game and by demonstrating and encouraging behaviors that express these values at all times.

These are your responsibilities as a coach. But coaching becomes even more complicated when your child is a player on the team you coach. If this is the case, you'll have to take into account your roles as both a coach and a parent and think about how those roles relate to each other.

Coaching Your Own Child

Many coaches are parents, but the two roles should not be confused. Unlike your role as a parent, as a coach you are responsible not only to yourself and your child but also to the organization, all the players on the team (including your child), and their parents. Because of this additional responsibility, your behavior on the volleyball court will be different from your behavior at home, and your son or daughter may not understand why.

For example, imagine the confusion of a young boy who is the center of his parents' attention at home but is barely noticed by his father/coach in the sport setting. Or consider the mixed signals received by a young girl whose volleyball skill is constantly evaluated by a mother/coach who otherwise rarely comments on her daughter's activities. You need to explain to your son or daughter your new responsibilities and how they will affect your relationship when coaching.

Take the following steps to avoid problems in coaching your child:

- Ask your child if he or she wants you to coach the team.
- Explain why you wish to be involved with the team.
- Discuss with your child how your interactions will change when you take on the role of coach at practices or games.
- Limit your coaching behavior to when you are in the coaching role.
- Avoid parenting during practice or game situations, to keep your role clear in your child's mind.
- Reaffirm your love for your child, irrespective of his or her performance on the volleyball court.

Now let's look at some of the qualities that will help you become an effective coach.

Five Tools of an Effective Coach

Have you purchased the traditional coaching tools—things like whistles, coaching clothes, sport shoes, and a clipboard? They'll help you coach, but to be a successful coach you'll need five other tools that cannot be bought. These tools are available only through self-examination and hard work; they're easy to remember with the acronym COACH:

C – Comprehension
O – Outlook
A – Affection
C – Character
H – Humor

Comprehension

Comprehension of the rules, tactics, and skills of volleyball is required. You must understand the basic elements of the sport. To assist you in learning about the game, we describe rules, tactics, and skills in chapters 7 and 8. We also provide season plans in chapter 9.

To improve your comprehension of volleyball, take the following steps:

- Read the sport-specific section of this book in chapters 7, 8, and 9.
- Consider reading other volleyball coaching books, including those available from the American Sport Education Program (ASEP).
- Contact youth volleyball organizations.
- Attend volleyball clinics.
- Talk with more experienced coaches.
- Observe local college, high school, and youth volleyball games.
- Watch volleyball games on television.

In addition to having volleyball knowledge, you must implement proper training and safety methods so your players can participate with little risk of injury. Even then, injuries may occur. And more often than not, you'll be the first person responding to your players' injuries, so be sure you understand the basic emergency care procedures described in chapter 3. Also, read in that chapter how to handle more serious sport injury situations.

Outlook

This coaching tool refers to your perspective and goals—what you are seeking as a coach. The most common coaching objectives are to (a) have fun; (b) help players develop their physical, mental, and social skills; and (c) win. Thus your *outlook* involves the priorities you set, your planning, and your vision for the future.

While all coaches focus on competition, we want you to focus on *positive* competition, keeping the pursuit of victory in perspective by making decisions that first are in the best interest of the players and second will help to win the game.

So how do you know if your outlook and priorities are in order? Here's a little test for you:

Which situation would you be most proud of?

a. Knowing that each participant enjoyed playing volleyball.

b. Seeing that all players improved their volleyball skills.

c. Winning the league championship.

Which statement best reflects your thoughts about sport?

a. If it isn't fun, don't do it.

b. Everyone should learn something every day.

c. Sport isn't fun if you don't win.

How would you like your players to remember you?

a. As a coach who was fun to play for.

b. As a coach who provided a good base of fundamental skills.

c. As a coach who had a winning record.

Which would you most like to hear a parent of a player on your team say?

a. Mike really had a good time playing volleyball this year.

b. Nicole learned some important lessons playing volleyball this year.

c. Willie played on the first-place volleyball team this year.

Which of the following would be the most rewarding moment of your season?

a. Having your team not want to stop playing, even after practice is over.

b. Seeing one of your players finally master the skill of forearm passing.

c. Winning the league championship.

Look over your answers. If you most often selected "a" responses, then having fun is most important to you. A majority of "b" answers suggests that skill development is what attracts you to coaching. And if "c" was your most frequent response, winning is tops on your list of coaching priorities. If your priorities are in order, your players' well-being will take precedence over your team's win-loss record every time.

The American Sport Education Program (ASEP) has a motto that will help you keep your outlook in line with the best interests of the kids on your team. It summarizes in four words all you need to remember when establishing your coaching priorities:

Athletes First, Winning Second

This motto recognizes that striving to win is an important, even vital, part of sports. But it emphatically states that no efforts in striving to win should be made at the expense of the athletes' well-being, development, and enjoyment.

Take the following actions to better define your outlook:

1. Determine your priorities for the season.
2. Prepare for situations that challenge your priorities.
3. Set goals for yourself and your players that are consistent with those priorities.
4. Plan how you and your players can best attain those goals.
5. Review your goals frequently to be sure that you are staying on track.

Affection

This is another vital tool you will want to have in your coaching kit: a genuine concern for the young people you coach. It involves having a love for kids, a desire to share with them your love and knowledge of volleyball, and the patience and understanding that allow each individual playing for you to grow from his or her involvement in sport.

You can demonstrate your affection and patience in many ways, including these:

- Make an effort to get to know each player on your team.
- Treat each player as an individual.
- Empathize with players trying to learn new and difficult skills.
- Treat players as you would like to be treated under similar circumstances.
- Be in control of your emotions.
- Show your enthusiasm for being involved with your team.
- Keep an upbeat and positive tone in all of your communications.

Character

The fact that you have decided to coach young volleyball players probably means that you think participation in sport is important. But whether or not that participation develops character in your players depends as much on you as it does on the sport itself. How can you build character in your players?

Having good character means modeling appropriate behaviors for sport and life. That means more than just saying the right things. What you say and what you do must match. There is no place in coaching for the "Do as I say, not as I do" philosophy. Challenge, support, encourage, and reward every youngster, and your players will be more likely to accept, even celebrate, their differences. Be in control before, during, and after all practices and contests. And don't be afraid to admit that you were wrong. No one is perfect!

Consider the following steps to being a good role model:

- Take stock of your strengths and weaknesses.
- Build on your strengths.
- Set goals for yourself to improve upon those areas you would not like to see copied.
- If you slip up, apologize to your team and to yourself. You'll do better next time.

Humor

Humor is an often-overlooked coaching tool. For our use it means having the ability to laugh at yourself and with your players during practices and contests. Nothing helps balance the tone of a serious skill-learning session like a chuckle or two. And a sense of humor puts in perspective the many mistakes your players will make. So don't get upset over each miscue or respond negatively to erring players. Allow your players and yourself to enjoy the ups, and don't dwell on the downs.

Here are some tips for injecting humor into your practices:

- Make practices fun by including a variety of activities.
- Keep all players involved in games and skill practices.
- Consider laughter by your players a sign of enjoyment not of waning discipline.
- Smile!

chapter 2

Communicating As a Coach

In chapter 1 you learned about the tools needed to COACH: Comprehension, Outlook, Affection, Character, and Humor. These are essentials for effective coaching; without them, you'd have a difficult time getting started. But none of the tools will work if you don't know how to use them with your athletes—and this requires skillful communication. This chapter examines what communication is and how you can become a more effective communicator-coach.

What's Involved in Communication?

Coaches often mistakenly believe that communication involves only instructing players to do something, but verbal commands are only a small part of the communication process. More than half of what is communicated is nonverbal. So remember when you are coaching: Actions speak louder than words.

Communication in its simplest form involves two people: a sender and a receiver. The sender transmits the message verbally, through facial expressions, and possibly through body language. Once the message is sent, the receiver must assimilate it successfully. A receiver who fails to attend or listen will miss parts, if not all, of the message.

How Can I Send More Effective Messages?

Young athletes often have little understanding of the rules and skills of volleyball and probably even less confidence in playing it. So they need accurate, understandable, and supportive messages to help them along. That's why your verbal and nonverbal messages are so important.

Verbal Messages

"Sticks and stones may break my bones, but words will never hurt me" isn't true. Spoken words can have a strong and long-lasting effect. And coaches' words are particularly influential because youngsters place great importance on what coaches say. Perhaps you, like many former youth sport participants, have a difficult time remembering much of anything you were told by your elementary school teachers, but you can still recall several specific things your coaches at that level said to you. Such is the lasting effect of a coach's comments to a player.

Whether you are correcting misbehavior, teaching a player how to hit the ball, or praising a player for good effort, you should consider a number of things when sending a message verbally. They include the following:

- Be positive and honest.
- State it clearly and simply.
- Say it loud enough, and say it again.
- Be consistent.

Be Positive and Honest

Nothing turns people off like hearing someone nag all the time, and athletes react similarly to a coach who gripes constantly. Kids particularly need encouragement because they often doubt their ability to perform in a sport. So look for and tell your players what they did well.

But don't cover up poor or incorrect play with rosy words of praise. Kids know all too well when they've erred, and no cheerfully expressed cliche can undo their mistakes. If you fail to acknowledge players' errors, your athletes will think you are a phony.

A good way to correct a performance error is to first point out what the athlete did correctly. Then explain in a positive way what he or she is doing wrong and show him or her how to correct it. Finish by encouraging the athlete and emphasizing the correct performance.

Be sure not to follow a positive statement with the word *but*. For example, don't say, "That was a good approach on your attack, Kelly. But remember to contact the ball at the peak of your jump." Saying it this way causes many kids to ignore the positive statement and focus on the negative one. Instead, say something like, "That was a good approach on your attack, Kelly. And if you contact the ball at the peak of your jump, you'll be able to get more zip on the ball and get a better angle on your spike. That was right on target. That's the way to go."

State It Clearly and Simply

Positive and honest messages are good, but only if expressed directly in words your players understand. "Beating around the bush" is ineffective and inefficient. And if you do ramble, your players will miss the point of your message and probably lose interest. Here are some tips for saying things clearly:

- Organize your thoughts before speaking to your athletes.
- Explain things thoroughly, but don't bore them with long-winded monologues.
- Use language your players can understand. However, avoid trying to be hip by using their age group's slang vocabulary.

Say It Loud Enough, and Say It Again

Talk to your team in a voice that all members can hear and interpret. A crisp, vigorous voice commands attention and respect; garbled and weak speech is tuned out. It's OK, in fact, appropriate, to soften your voice when speaking to a player individually about a personal problem. But most of the time your messages will be for all your players to hear, so make sure they can! An enthusiastic voice also motivates players and tells them you enjoy being their coach. A word of caution, however: Don't dominate the setting with a booming voice that distracts attention from players' performances.

Sometimes what you say, even if stated loudly and clearly, won't sink in the first time. This may be particularly true when young athletes hear words they don't understand. To avoid boring repetition and yet still get your message across, say the same thing in a slightly different way. For instance, you might first tell your players, "Remember when you're passing to keep a flat surface with your forearms!" If they don't appear to understand, you might say, "When your forearms are flat, you can direct the pass better. Otherwise the ball could bounce off in just about any direction." The second form of the message may get through to players who missed it the first time around.

Be Consistent

People often say things in ways that imply a different message. For example, a touch of sarcasm added to the words "Way to go!" sends an entirely different message than the words themselves suggest. Avoid sending such mixed messages. Keep the tone of your voice consistent with the words you use. And don't say something one day and contradict it the next; players will get their wires crossed.

Nonverbal Messages

Just as you should be consistent in the tone of voice and words you use, you should also keep your verbal and nonverbal messages consistent. An extreme example of failing to do this would be shaking your head, indicating disapproval, while at the same time telling a player "Nice try." Which is the player to believe, your gesture or your words?

Messages can be sent nonverbally in a number of ways. Facial expressions and body language are just two of the more obvious forms of nonverbal signals that can help you when you coach.

Facial Expressions

The look on a person's face is the quickest clue to what he or she thinks or feels. Your players know this, so they will study your face, looking for any sign that will tell them more than the words you say. Don't try to fool them by putting on a happy or blank "mask." They'll see through it, and you'll lose credibility.

Serious, stone-faced expressions are no help to kids who need cues as to how they are performing. They will just assume you're unhappy or disinterested. Don't be afraid to smile. A smile from a coach can give a great boost to an unsure athlete. Plus, a smile lets your players know that you are happy coaching them. But don't overdo it, or your players won't be able to tell when you are genuinely pleased by something they've done or when you are just putting on a smiling face.

Body Language

What would your players think you were feeling if you came to practice slouched over, with your head down and shoulders slumped? Tired? Bored? Unhappy? What would they think you were feeling if you watched them during a contest with your hands on your hips, your jaws clenched, and your face reddened? Upset with them? Disgusted with an official? Mad at a fan? Probably some or all of these things would enter your players' minds. And none of these impressions is the kind you want your players to have of you. That's why you should carry yourself in a pleasant, confident, and vigorous manner. Such a posture not only projects happiness with your coaching role but also provides a good example for your young players, who may model your behavior.

Physical contact can also be a very important use of body language. A handshake, a pat on the head, an arm around the shoulder, or even a big hug are effective ways of showing approval, concern, affection, and joy to your players. Youngsters are especially in need of this type of nonverbal message. Keep within the obvious moral and legal limits, of course, but don't be reluctant to touch your players, sending a message that can only truly be expressed in that way.

How Can I Improve My Receiving Skills?

Now, let's examine the other half of the communication process—receiving messages. Too often very good senders are very poor receivers of messages. But as a coach of young athletes, you must be able to fulfill both roles effectively.

The requirements for receiving messages are quite simple, but receiving skills are perhaps less satisfying and therefore underdeveloped compared to sending skills. People seem to naturally enjoy hearing themselves talk more than hearing others talk. But if you read about the keys to receiving messages and make a strong effort to use them with your players, you'll be surprised by what you've been missing.

Attention!

First, you must pay attention; you must want to hear what others have to communicate to you. That's not always easy when you're busy coaching and have many things competing for your attention. But in one-on-one or team meetings with players, you must really focus on what they are telling you, both verbally and nonverbally. You'll be amazed at the little signals you pick up. Not only will such focused attention help you catch every word your players say, but also you'll notice your players' moods and physical states. In addition, you'll get an idea of your players' feelings toward you and other players on the team.

Listen CARE-FULLY

How we receive messages from others, perhaps more than anything else we do, demonstrates how much we care for the sender and what that person has to tell us. If you care little for your players or have little regard for what they have to say, it will show in how you attend and listen to them. Check yourself. Do you find your mind wandering to what you are going to do after practice while one of your players is talking to you? Do you frequently have to ask your players, "What did you say?" If so, you need to work on your receiving mechanics of attending and listening. But perhaps the most critical question you should ask yourself if you find that you're missing the messages your players send is this: Do I care?

Providing Feedback

So far we've discussed separately the sending and receiving of messages. But we all know that senders and receivers switch roles several times during an interaction. One person initiates a communication by sending a message to another person, who then receives the message. The receiver then switches roles and becomes the sender by responding to the person who sent the initial message. These verbal and nonverbal responses are called *feedback*.

Your players will be looking to you for feedback all the time. They will want to know how you think they are performing, what you think of their ideas, and whether their efforts please you. Obviously, you can respond in many different ways. How you respond will strongly affect your players. They will respond most favorably to positive feedback.

Praising players when they have performed or behaved well is an effective way of getting them to repeat (or try to repeat) that behavior in the future. And positive feedback for effort is an especially effective way to motivate youngsters to work on difficult skills. So rather than shouting and providing negative feedback to players who have made mistakes, try offering players positive feedback, letting them know what they did correctly and how they can improve.

Sometimes just the way you word feedback can make it more positive than negative. For example, instead of saying, "Don't hit the ball that way," you might say, "Hit the ball this way." Then your players will be focusing on what to do instead of what not to do.

You can give positive feedback verbally and nonverbally. Telling a player, especially in front of teammates, that he or she has performed well is a great way to boost the confidence of a youngster. And a pat on the back or a handshake can be a very tangible way of communicating your recognition of a player's performance.

Who Else Do I Need to Communicate With?

Coaching involves not only sending and receiving messages and providing proper feedback to players but also interacting with parents, fans, game officials, and opposing coaches. If you don't communicate effectively with these groups of people, your coaching career will be unpleasant and short-lived. So try the following suggestions for communicating with these groups.

Parents

A player's parents need to be assured that their son or daughter is under the direction of a coach who is both knowledgeable about the sport and concerned about the youngster's well-being. You can put their worries to rest by holding a preseason parent-orientation meeting in which you describe your background and your approach to coaching.

If parents contact you with a concern during the season, listen to them closely and try to offer positive responses. If you need to communicate with parents, catch them after a practice, give them a phone call, or send a note through the mail. Messages sent to parents through players are too often lost, misinterpreted, or forgotten.

Fans

The stands probably won't be overflowing at your contests, but that only means that you'll more easily hear the few fans who criticize your coaching. When you hear something negative said about the job you're doing, don't respond. Keep calm, consider whether the message had any value, and if not, forget it. Acknowledging critical, unwarranted comments from a fan during a contest will only encourage others to voice their opinions. So put away your rabbit ears and communicate to fans through your actions that you are a confident, competent coach.

Prepare your players for fans' criticisms. Tell them it is you, not the spectators, they should listen to. If you notice that one of your players is rattled by a fan's comment, reassure the player that your evaluation is more objective and favorable—and the one that counts.

Contest Officials

How you communicate with officials will have a great influence on the way your players behave toward them. Therefore, you need to set an example. Greet officials with a handshake, an introduction, and perhaps some casual conversation about the upcoming contest. Indicate your respect for them before, during, and after the contest. Don't make nasty remarks, shout, or use disrespectful body gestures. Your players will see you do it, and they'll get the idea that such behavior is appropriate. Plus, if the official hears or sees you, the communication between the two of you will break down.

Opposing Coaches

Make an effort to visit with the coach of the opposing team before the game. During the game, don't get into a personal feud with the opposing coach. Remember, it's the kids, not the coaches, who are competing. And by getting along well with the opposing coach, you'll show your players that competition involves cooperation.

chapter 3

Providing for Players' Safety

One of your players reacts quickly to the ball, diving to dig a spike hit toward the sideline. Incredibly, your player digs the ball to a teammate and saves the point. But just as you turn to praise the gutsy play, you see that the player is still down on the court. She is clutching her elbow and seems to be in pain. What do you do?

No coach wants to see players get hurt. But injury remains a reality of sport participation; consequently, you must be prepared to provide first aid when injuries occur and to protect yourself against unjustified lawsuits. Fortunately, there are many preventive measures coaches can institute to reduce the risk. In this chapter we describe

- steps you can take to prevent injuries,
- first aid and emergency responses for when injuries occur, and
- your legal responsibilities as a coach.

The Game Plan for Safety

You can't prevent all injuries from happening, but you can take preventive measures that give your players the best possible chance for injury-free participation. In creating the safest possible environment for your athletes, we'll explore what you can do in these six areas:

- Preseason physical examinations
- Physical conditioning
- Equipment and facilities inspection
- Matching athletes and inherent risks
- Proper supervision and record keeping
- Environmental conditions

We'll begin with what should take place *before* the season begins: the preseason physical examination.

Preseason Physical Examination

We recommend that your players have a physical examination before participating in volleyball. The exam should address the most likely areas of medical concern and identify youngsters at high risk. We also suggest that you have players' parents or guardians sign a participation agreement form and a release form to allow their children to be treated in case of an emergency.

Physical Conditioning

Players need to be in, or get in, shape to play the game at the level expected. To do so, they'll need to have adequate *cardiorespiratory fitness* and *muscular fitness.*

Cardiorespiratory fitness involves the body's ability to store and use oxygen and fuels efficiently to power muscle contractions. As players get in better shape, their bodies are able to more efficiently deliver oxygen and fuels to muscles and carry off carbon dioxides and other wastes. Volleyball involves lots of movement and the ability to make short bursts throughout a game.

An advantage of teaching volleyball with the games approach is that kids are active during almost the entire practice; there is no standing around in lines, watching teammates take part in drills. Players will be attaining higher levels of cardiorespiratory fitness as the season progresses simply by taking part in practice. However, watch closely for signs of low levels of cardiorespiratory fitness; don't let your athletes do too much until they're fit. You might privately counsel youngsters who appear overly winded, suggesting that they train outside of practice to increase their fitness.

Muscular fitness encompasses strength, muscle endurance, power, speed, and flexibility. This type of fitness is affected by physical maturity, as well as strength training and other types of training. Your players will likely exhibit a relatively wide range of muscular fitness. Those who have greater muscular fitness will be able to run faster and hit the ball harder. They will also sustain fewer muscular injuries, and any injuries that do occur will tend to be more minor in nature. And in case of injury, recovery rate is accelerated in those with higher levels of muscular fitness.

Two other components of fitness and injury prevention are the warm-up and the cool-down. Although young bodies are generally very limber, they, too, can get tight from inactivity. The warm-up should address each muscle group and get the heart rate elevated in preparation for strenuous activity. Have players warm up for five minutes by playing easy games and stretching.

As practice winds down, slow players' heart rates with an easy jog or walk. Then have players stretch for five minutes to help avoid stiff muscles and make them less tight before the next practice or contest.

Equipment and Facilities Inspection

Another way to prevent injuries is to examine regularly the court on which your players practice and play. Remove hazards, report conditions you cannot remedy, and request maintenance as necessary. If unsafe conditions exist, either make adaptations to avoid risk to your players' safety or stop the practice or game until safe conditions have been restored.

Player Match-Ups and Inherent Risks

We recommend you group teams in two-year age ranges if possible. You'll encounter fewer mismatches in physical maturation with narrow age ranges. Even so, two 12-year-old boys might differ by 90 pounds in weight, a foot in height, and three or four years in emotional and intellectual maturity. This presents dangers for the less mature. Whenever possible, match players against opponents of similar size and physical maturity. Such an approach gives smaller, less mature youngsters a better chance to succeed and avoid injury while providing more mature players with a greater challenge. Closely supervise games so that the more mature do not put the less mature at undue risk.

Proper matching helps protect you from certain liability concerns. But you must also warn players of the inherent risks involved in playing volleyball because "failure to warn" is one of the most successful arguments in lawsuits against coaches. So, thoroughly explain the inherent risks of volleyball, and make sure each player knows, understands, and appreciates those risks.

The preseason parent-orientation meeting is a good opportunity to explain the risks of the sport to both parents and players. It is also a good occasion on which to have both the players and their parents sign waivers releasing you from liability should an injury occur. Such waivers do not relieve you of responsibility for your players' well-being, but they are recommended by lawyers.

Proper Supervision and Record Keeping

To ensure players' safety, you will need to provide both general supervision and specific supervision. *General supervision* is being in the area of activity so that you can see and hear what is happening. You should be

- immediately accessible to the activity and able to oversee the entire activity,
- alert to conditions that may be dangerous to players and ready to take action to protect them, and
- able to react immediately and appropriately to emergencies.

Specific supervision is direct supervision of an activity at practice. For example, you should provide specific supervision when you teach new skills and continue it until your athletes understand the requirements of the activity, the risks involved, and their own ability to perform in light of these risks. You need to also provide specific supervision when you notice either players breaking rules or a change in the condition of your athletes.

As a general rule, the more dangerous the activity, the more specific the supervision required. This suggests that more specific supervision is required with younger and less experienced athletes.

As part of your supervision duty, you are expected to foresee potentially dangerous situations and to be positioned to help prevent them from occurring. This requires that you know volleyball well, especially the rules that are intended to provide for safety. Prohibit dangerous horseplay, and, if you play outside, hold practices and games only under safe weather conditions. These specific supervisory activities applied consistently will make the play environment safer for your players and will help protect you from liability if a mishap does occur.

For further protection, keep records of your season plans, practice plans, and players' injuries. Season and practice plans come in handy when you need evidence that players have been taught certain skills, whereas accurate, detailed injury-report forms offer protection against unfounded lawsuits. Ask for these forms from your sponsoring organization (appendix A has a sample injury-report form), and hold onto these records for several years so that an "old volleyball injury" of a former player doesn't come back to haunt you.

Environmental Conditions

Most problems due to environmental factors are related to excessive heat, though you should also consider other environmental factors such as severe weather and pollution. A little thought about the potential problems and a little effort to ensure adequate protection for your athletes will prevent most serious emergencies that are related to environmental conditions. Heat can be a factor for both indoor and outdoor play. Information on cold, severe weather, and air pollution are pertinent to teams that practice or play outdoors.

Heat

On hot, humid days the body has difficulty cooling itself. Because the air is already saturated with water vapor (humidity), sweat doesn't evaporate as easily. Therefore, body sweat is a less effective cooling agent, and the body retains extra heat. Hot, humid environments make athletes prone to heat exhaustion and heatstroke (see more on these in "Serious Injuries" on page 29). And if *you* think it's hot or humid, it's worse on the kids—not only because they're more active but also because youngsters under the age of 12 have a more difficult time than adults regulating their body temperature. To provide for players' safety in hot or humid conditions, take the following preventive measures.

⊙ **Monitor weather conditions and adjust practices accordingly.** Figure 3.1 shows the specific air temperatures and humidity percentages that can be hazardous.

⊙ **Acclimatize players to exercising in high heat and humidity.** Athletes can make adjustments to high heat and humidity over 7 to 10 days. During this time, hold practices at low to moderate activity levels and give the players water breaks every 20 minutes.

⊙ **Switch to light clothing.** Players should wear shorts and white T-shirts.

⊙ **Identify and monitor players who are prone to heat illness.** Players who are overweight, heavily muscled, or out of shape will be more prone to heat illness, as are athletes who work excessively hard or who have suffered heat illness before. Closely monitor these athletes and give them water breaks every 15 to 20 minutes.

⊙ **Make sure athletes replace water lost through sweat.** Encourage your players to drink one liter of water each day outside of practice and contest times, to drink eight ounces of water every 20 minutes during practice or competition, and to drink four to eight ounces of water 20 minutes before practice or competition.

⊙ **Replenish electrolytes lost through sweat.** Sodium (salt) and potassium are lost through sweat. The best way to replace these nutrients is by eating a normal diet that contains fresh fruits and vegetables. Bananas are a good source of potassium. The normal American diet contains plenty of salt, so players don't need to go overboard in salting their food to replace lost sodium.

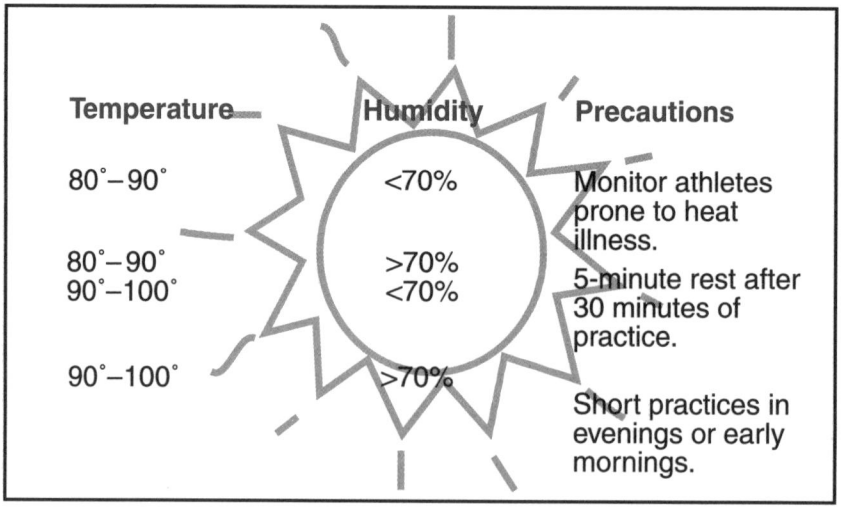

Figure 3.1 Warm-weather precautions.

Water, Water Everywhere

Encourage players to drink plenty of water before, during, and after practice. Because water makes up 45 percent to 65 percent of a youngster's body weight and water weighs about a pound per pint, the loss of even a little bit of water can have severe consequences for the body's systems. And it doesn't have to be hot and humid for players to become dehydrated. Nor do players have to feel thirsty; in fact, by the time they are aware of their thirst, they are long overdue for a drink.

Cold

Again, this pertains to teams that practice and play outdoors. When a person is exposed to cold weather, the body temperature starts to drop below normal. To counteract this, the body shivers and reduces the blood flow to gain or conserve heat. But no matter how effective the body's natural heating mechanism is, the body will withstand cold temperatures better if it is prepared to handle them. To reduce the risk of cold-related illnesses, make sure players wear appropriate protective clothing, and keep them active to maintain body heat. Also monitor the windchill (see figure 3.2).

Wind speed (mph)	Temperature (°F)								
	0	5	10	15	20	25	30	35	40
	Flesh may freeze within 1 minute								
40	-55	-45	-35	-30	-20	-15	-5	0	10
35	-50	-40	-35	-30	-20	-10	-5	5	10
30	-50	-40	-30	-25	-20	-10	0	5	10
25	-45	-35	-30	-20	-15	-5	0	10	15
20	-35	-30	-25	-15	-10	0	5	10	20
15	-30	-25	-20	-10	-5	0	10	15	25
10	-20	-15	-10	0	5	10	15	20	30
5	-5	0	5	10	15	20	25	30	35

Windchill temperature (°F)

Figure 3.2 Windchill factor index.

Severe Weather

Severe weather refers to a host of potential dangers, including lightning storms, tornadoes, hail, heavy rains, and so on.

Lightning is of special concern for outdoor practices and competitions because it can come up quickly and can cause great harm or even kill. For each 5-second count from the flash of lightning to the bang of thunder, lightning is one mile away. A flash-bang of 10 seconds means lightning is two miles away; a flash-bang of 15 seconds indicates lightning is three miles away. A practice or competition should be stopped for the day if lightning is three miles away or less (15 seconds or less from flash to bang).

Safe places in which to take cover when lightning strikes are fully enclosed metal vehicles with the windows up, enclosed buildings, and low ground (under cover of bushes, if possible). It's *not* safe to be near metallic objects—flag poles, fences, light poles, metal bleachers, and so on. Also avoid trees, water, and open fields.

Cancel practice when under either a tornado watch or warning. If for some reason you are practicing or competing when a tornado is nearby, you should get inside a building if possible. If not, lie in a ditch or other low-lying area or crouch near a strong building, and use your arms to protect your head and neck.

The keys to handling severe weather are caution and prudence. Don't try to get that last 10 minutes of practice in if lightning is on the horizon. Don't continue to play in heavy rains. Many storms can strike both quickly and ferociously. Respect the weather and play it safe.

Air Pollution

Poor air quality and smog can present real dangers to your players. Both short- and long-term lung damage are possible from participating in unsafe air. While it's true that participating in clean air is not possible in many areas, restricting activity is recommended when the air-quality ratings are worse than moderate or when there is a smog alert. Your local health department or air-quality control board can inform you of the air-quality ratings for your area and when restricting activities is recommended.

Responding to Players' Injuries

No matter how good and thorough your prevention program is, injuries may occur. When injury does strike, chances are you will be the one in charge. The severity and nature of the injury will determine how actively involved you'll be in treating the injury. But regardless of how seriously a player is hurt, it is your responsibility to know what steps to take. So let's look at how you should prepare to provide basic emergency care to your injured athletes and take the appropriate action when an injury does occur.

Being Prepared

Being prepared to provide basic emergency care involves three steps: being trained in cardiopulmonary resuscitation (CPR) and first aid, having an appropriately stocked first-aid kit on hand at practices and games, and having an emergency plan.

CPR and First-Aid Training

We recommend that all coaches receive CPR and first aid training from a nationally recognized organization (the National Safety Council, the American Heart Association, the American Red Cross, or the American Sport Education Program). You should be certified based on a practical test and a written test of knowledge. CPR training should include pediatric and adult basic life support and obstructed airway procedures.

First-Aid Kit

A well-stocked first-aid kit should include the following:

- List of emergency phone numbers
- Change for a pay phone
- Face shield (for rescue breathing and CPR)
- Bandage scissors
- Plastic bags for crushed ice
- 3-inch and 4-inch elastic wraps
- Triangular bandages
- Sterile gauze pads (3-inch and 4-inch squares)
- Saline solution for eyes
- Contact lens case
- Mirror
- Penlight
- Tongue depressors
- Cotton swabs

- Butterfly strips
- Bandage strips—assorted sizes
- Alcohol or peroxide
- Antibacterial soap
- First aid cream or antibacterial ointment
- Petroleum jelly
- Tape adherent and tape remover
- 1 $\frac{1}{2}$-inch, white athletic tape
- Prewrap
- Sterile gauze rolls
- Insect-sting kit
- Safety pins
- $\frac{1}{8}$-inch, $\frac{1}{4}$-inch, and $\frac{1}{2}$-inch foam rubber
- Disposable surgical gloves
- Thermometer

Emergency Plan

An emergency plan is the final step in preparing to take appropriate action for severe or serious injuries. The plan calls for three steps:

1. **Evaluate the injured player.** Your CPR and first-aid training will guide you here.

2. **Call the appropriate medical personnel.** If possible, delegate the responsibility of seeking medical help to another calm and responsible adult who is on hand for all practices and games. Write out a list of emergency phone numbers and keep it with you at practices and games. Include the following phone numbers:

- Rescue unit
- Hospital
- Physician
- Police
- Fire department

Take each athlete's emergency information to every practice and game (see appendix B). This information includes the person to contact in case of an emergency, what types of medications the athlete is using, what types of drugs he or she is allergic to, and so on.

Give an emergency response card (see appendix C) to the contact person calling for emergency assistance. This provides the information the contact person needs to convey and will help keep the person calm, knowing that everything he or she needs to communicate is on the card. Also complete an injury-report form (see appendix A) and keep it on file for any injury that occurs.

3. **Provide first aid.** If medical personnel are not on hand at the time of the injury, you should provide first-aid care to the extent of your qualifications. Again, while your CPR and first-aid training will guide you here, the following are important guidelines:

- Do not move the injured athlete if the injury is to the head, neck, or back; if a large joint (ankle, knee, elbow, shoulder) is dislocated; or if the pelvis, a rib, or an arm or leg is fractured.
- Calm the injured athlete and keep others away from him or her as much as possible.
- Evaluate whether the athlete's breathing is stopped or irregular, and if necessary, clear the airway with your fingers.
- Administer artificial respiration if the athlete's breathing has stopped. Administer CPR if the athlete's circulation has stopped.
- Remain with the athlete until medical personnel arrive.

Emergency Steps

Your emergency plan should follow this sequence:

1. Check the athlete's level of consciousness.
2. Send a contact person to call the appropriate medical personnel and to call the athlete's parents.
3. Send someone to wait for the rescue team and direct them to the injured athlete.
4. Assess the injury.
5. Administer first aid.
6. Assist emergency medical personnel in preparing the athlete for transportation to a medical facility.
7. Appoint someone to go with the athlete if the parents are not available. This person should be responsible, calm, and familiar with the athlete. Assistant coaches or parents are best for this job.
8. Complete an injury-report form while the incident is fresh in your mind (see appendix A).

Taking Appropriate Action

Proper CPR and first-aid training, a well-stocked first aid kit, and an emergency plan help prepare you to take appropriate action when an injury occurs. We spoke in the previous section about the importance of providing first aid *to the extent of your qualifications.* Don't "play doctor" with injuries; sort out minor injuries that you can treat from those for which you need to call for medical assistance.

Next we'll look at taking the appropriate action for minor injuries and more serious injuries.

Minor Injuries

Although no injury seems minor to the person experiencing it, most injuries are neither life-threatening nor severe enough to restrict participation. When such injuries occur, you can take an active role in their initial treatment.

Scrapes and Cuts. When one of your players has an open wound, the first thing you should do is put on a pair of disposable surgical gloves or some other effective blood barrier. Then follow these four steps:

1. *Stop the bleeding* by applying direct pressure with a clean dressing to the wound and elevating it. The player may be able to apply this pressure while you put on your gloves. Do not remove the dressing if it becomes soaked with blood. Instead, place an additional dressing on top of the one already in place. If bleeding continues, elevate the injured area above the heart and maintain pressure.

2. *Cleanse the wound* thoroughly once the bleeding is controlled. A good rinsing with a forceful stream of water, and perhaps light scrubbing with soap, will help prevent infection.

3. *Protect the wound* with sterile gauze or a bandage strip. If the player continues to participate, apply protective padding over the injured area.

4. *Remove and dispose of gloves* carefully to prevent you or anyone else from coming into contact with blood.

For bloody noses not associated with serious facial injury, have the athlete sit and lean slightly forward. Then pinch the player's nostrils shut. If the bleeding continues after several minutes or if the athlete has a history of nosebleeds, seek medical assistance.

Treating Bloody Injuries

You shouldn't let a fear of acquired immune deficiency syndrome (AIDS) stop you from helping a player. You are only at risk if you allow contaminated blood to come in contact with an open wound, so the surgical disposable gloves that you wear will protect you from AIDS should one of your players carry this disease. Check with your director or your organization for more information about protecting yourself and your participants from AIDS.

Strains and Sprains. The physical demands of volleyball practices and games often result in injury to the muscles or tendons (strains) or to the ligaments (sprains). When your players suffer minor strains or sprains, immediately apply the PRICE method of injury care:

P – Protect the athlete and injured body part from further danger or trauma.

R – Rest the area to avoid further damage and foster healing.

I – Ice the area to reduce swelling and pain.

C – Compress the area by securing an ice bag in place with an elastic wrap.

E – Elevate the injury above heart level to keep the blood from pooling in the area.

Bumps and Bruises. Inevitably, volleyball players make contact with each other and with the floor or ground. If the force applied to a body part at impact is great enough, a bump or bruise will result. Many players continue playing with such sore spots, but if the bump or bruise is large and painful, you should act appropriately. Use the PRICE method for injury care and monitor the injury. If swelling, discoloration, and pain have lessened, the player may resume participation with protective padding; if not, the player should be examined by a physician.

Serious Injuries

Head, neck, and back injuries; fractures; and injuries that cause a player to lose consciousness are among a class of injuries that you cannot and should not try to treat yourself. In these cases you should follow the emergency plan outlined on page 27. We do want to examine more closely your role, however, in preventing and handling two heat illnesses: heat exhaustion and heatstroke.

Heat Exhaustion. Heat exhaustion is a shocklike condition caused by dehydration and electrolyte depletion. Symptoms include headache, nausea, dizziness, chills, fatigue, and extreme thirst (see figure 3.3 for heat exhaustion and heatstroke symptoms). Profuse sweating is a key sign of heat exhaustion. Other signs include pale, cool, and clammy skin; rapid, weak pulse; loss of coordination; and dilated pupils.

A player suffering from heat exhaustion should rest in a cool, shaded area; drink cool water; and have ice applied to the neck, back, or abdomen to help cool the body. You may have to administer CPR if necessary or send for emergency medical assistance if the athlete doesn't recover or his or her condition worsens. Under no conditions should the athlete return to activity that day or before he or she regains all the weight lost through sweat. If the player has to see a physician, he or she shouldn't return to the team until he or she has a written release from the physician.

Heatstroke. Heatstroke is a life-threatening condition in which the body stops sweating and body temperature rises dangerously high. It occurs when dehydration causes a malfunction in the body's temperature control center in the brain. Symptoms include the feeling of being on fire (extremely hot), nausea, confusion, irritability, and fatigue. Signs include hot, dry, and flushed or red skin (this is a key sign); lack of sweat; rapid pulse; rapid breathing; constricted pupils; vomiting; diarrhea; and possibly seizures, unconsciousness, or respiratory or cardiac arrest. See figure 3.3 for heat exhaustion and heatstroke symptoms.

Send for emergency medical assistance immediately and have the player rest in a cool, shaded area. Remove excess clothing and equipment from the player, and cool the player's body with cool, wet towels or by pouring cool water over him or her. Apply ice packs to the armpits, neck, back, and abdomen, and between the legs. If the player is conscious, have him or her drink cool water. If the player is unconscious, place the player on his or her side to allow fluids and vomit to drain from the mouth.

An athlete who has suffered heatstroke may not return to the team until he or she has a written release from a physician.

Protecting Yourself

When one of your players is injured, naturally your first concern is his or her well-being. Your feelings for youngsters, after all, are what made

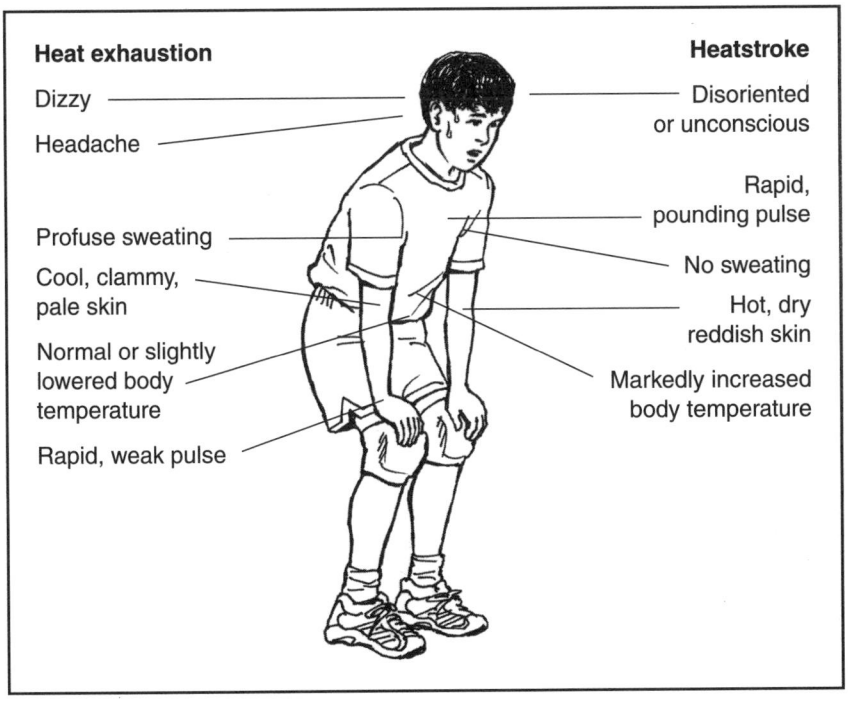

Figure 3.3 Signs and symptoms of heat exhaustion and heatstroke.

you decide to coach. Unfortunately, there is something else that you must consider: Can you be held liable for the injury?

From a legal standpoint, a coach has nine duties to fulfill. We've discussed all but planning in this chapter. The following is a summary of your legal duties:

1. Provide a safe environment.
2. Properly plan the activity.
3. Provide adequate and proper equipment.
4. Match, or equate, athletes.
5. Warn of inherent risks in the sport.
6. Supervise the activity closely.
7. Evaluate athletes for injury or incapacitation.
8. Know emergency procedures and first aid.
9. Keep adequate records.

Keep records of your season plan and practice plans and of players' injuries. Season and practice plans come in handy when you need evidence that players have been taught certain skills, and injury reports offer protection against unfounded lawsuits. Hold onto these records for several years so that an "old injury" of a former player doesn't come back to haunt you.

In addition to fulfilling these nine legal duties, you should check your organization's insurance coverage and your insurance coverage to make sure these policies will protect you from liability.

chapter 4

The Games Approach to Coaching Volleyball

Do you remember how as a kid you were taught by adults to play a sport, either in an organized sport program or physical education class? They probably taught you the basic skills using a series of drills that, if the truth be known, you found very boring. As you began to learn the basic skills, they eventually taught you the tactics of the game, showing you when to use these skills in various game situations. Do you remember how impatient you became during what seemed to be endless instruction, and how much you just wanted to play? Well, forget this traditional approach to teaching sport.

Now can you recall learning a sport by playing with a group of your friends in the neighborhood? You didn't learn the basic skills first; no time for that. You began playing immediately. If you didn't know the basic things to do, your friends told you quickly during the game so they could keep playing. Try to remember, because we're going to ask you to use a very similar approach to teaching volleyball to young people called the games approach, an approach we think knocks the socks off the traditional approach.

On the surface, it would seem to make sense to introduce volleyball by first teaching the basic skills of the sport and then the tactics of the game, but we've discovered that this approach has disadvantages. First, it teaches the skills of the sport out of the context of the game. Kids may learn to pass, set, spike, and dig, but they find it difficult to use these skills in the real game. This is because they do not yet understand the fundamental tactics of volleyball and do not appreciate how best to use their newfound skills.

Second, learning skills by doing drills outside of the context of the game is so-o-o-o boring. The single biggest turnoff about adults teaching kids sport is that we overorganize the instruction and deprive kids of their intrinsic desire to play the game.

As a coach we're asking that you teach volleyball the games approach way. Clear the traditional approach out of your mind. Once you fully understand the games approach, you'll quickly see its superiority in teaching volleyball. Not only will kids learn the game better but you and your players will have much more fun. And as a bonus, you'll have far fewer discipline problems.

With the games approach to teaching volleyball, we begin with a game. This will be a modified and much smaller game designed to suit the age and ability of the players. As the kids play in these "mini" games, you can begin to help them understand the nature of the game and to appreciate simple concepts of positioning and tactics. When your players understand what they must do in the game, they are then eager to develop the skills to play the game. Now that players are motivated to learn the skills, you can demonstrate the skills of the game, practice using game-like drills, and provide individual instruction by identifying players' errors and helping to correct them.

In the traditional approach to teaching sports, players do this:

Learn the skill → Learn the tactics → Play the game

In the games approach players do this:

Play the game → Learn the tactics → Learn the skill

In the past we have placed too much emphasis on the learning of skills and not enough on learning how to play skillfully—that is, how to use those skills in competition. The games approach, in contrast, emphasizes learning what to do first, then how to do it. Moreover—and this is a really important point—the games approach lets kids discover what to do in the game not by you telling them but by their experiencing it. What you do as an effective coach is help them discover what they've experienced.

In contrast to the "skill-drill-kill the enthusiasm" approach, the games approach is a guided discovery method of teaching. It empowers your kids to solve the problems that arise in the game, and that's a big part of the fun in learning a game.

Now let's look more closely at the games approach to see the four-step process for teaching volleyball:

1. Play a modified volleyball game.
2. Help the players discover what they need to do to play the game successfully.
3. Teach the skills of the game.
4. Practice the skills in another game.

Step 1. Play a Modified Volleyball Game

OK, it's the first day of practice; some of the kids are eager to get started, while others are obviously apprehensive. Some have rarely served a ball, most don't know the rules, and none know the positions in volleyball. What do you do?

If you use the traditional approach, you start with a little warm-up activity then line the players up for a simple hitting drill and go from there. With the games approach, you begin by playing a modified game that is developmentally appropriate for the level of the players and also designed to focus on learning a specific part of the game.

Modifying the game emphasizes a limited number of situations in the game. This is one way you guide your players to discover certain tactics in the game. For instance, you have your players play a 3 v 3 (three players versus three players) game on a 20- by 20-foot court. The objective of the game is to make forearm passes in setting up to attack.

Playing the game this way forces players to think about what they have to do to set up an effective attack.

Step 2. Help the Players Discover What They Need to Do

As your players are playing the game, look for the right spot to "freeze" the action, step in, and hold a brief question-and-answer session to discuss problems they were having in carrying out the goals of the game. You don't need to pop in on the first miscue, but if they repeat the same types of mental or physical mistakes a few times in a row, step in and ask them questions that relate to the aim of the game and the necessary skills required. The best time to interrupt the game is when you notice that they are having trouble carrying out the main goal, or aim, of the game. By stopping the game, freezing action, and asking questions, you'll help them understand

- what the aim of the game is,
- what they must do to achieve that aim, and
- what skills they must use to achieve that aim.

For example, if your players are playing a game in which the focus is on good forearm passes but they are having trouble making good passes, interrupt the action and ask the following questions:

Coach: What are you supposed to do in this game?

Players: Set up the attack with a good forearm pass.

Coach: How do you do that?

Players: Make a flat platform with the arms, keep arms parallel, have your belly button pointed toward the target.

Coach: Yes, and what else?

Players: You have to be able to get the pass, too.

Coach: OK. Flat platform, arms parallel, belly button pointed to the target. Why don't we practice forearm passes?

Through the modified game and skillful questioning on your part, your players realize that forearm passing is essential to their success in setting up the attack. Just as important, rather than *telling* them that forearm passing skills are critical, you led them to that discovery through a well-designed modified game and through questions. This questioning that leads to players' discovery is a crucial part of the games approach. Essentially you'll be asking your players—usually literally—"What do you need to do to succeed in this situation?"

Asking the right questions is a very important part of your teaching. At first asking questions will be difficult because your players have little or no experience with the game. And if you've learned sport through the traditional approach, you'll be tempted to tell your players how to play the game and not waste time asking them questions. Resist this powerful temptation to tell them what to do, and especially don't do so before they begin to play the game.

If your players have trouble understanding what to do, phrase your questions to let them choose between one option versus another. For example, if you ask them, "What's the best way to tip the ball?" and get answers such as "With your hand" or "Over the net," then ask, "Do you tip with an open hand or a clenched fist?"

Immediately following the question-and-answer session you will begin a skill practice, which is Step 3 of the four-step process.

Sometimes players simply need to have more time playing the game, or you may need to modify the game further so that it is even easier for them to discover what they are to do. It'll take more patience on your part, but it's a powerful way to learn. Don't be reluctant to change the numbers in the teams or some aspect of the structure of the game to aid this discovery.

Step 3. Teach the Skills of the Game

Only when your players recognize the skills they need to be successful in the game do you want to teach the specific skills through focused drills. This is when you use a more traditional approach to teaching sport skills called the "IDEA" approach, which we will describe in chapter 5.

Step 4. Practice the Skills in Another Game

Once the players have practiced the skill, you then put them in another game situation to let them practice the skill in the context of a game.

And that's the games approach. Your players will get to *play* more in practice, and once they learn how the skills fit into their performance and enjoyment of the game, they'll be more motivated to work on those skills, which will help them to be successful.

chapter 5

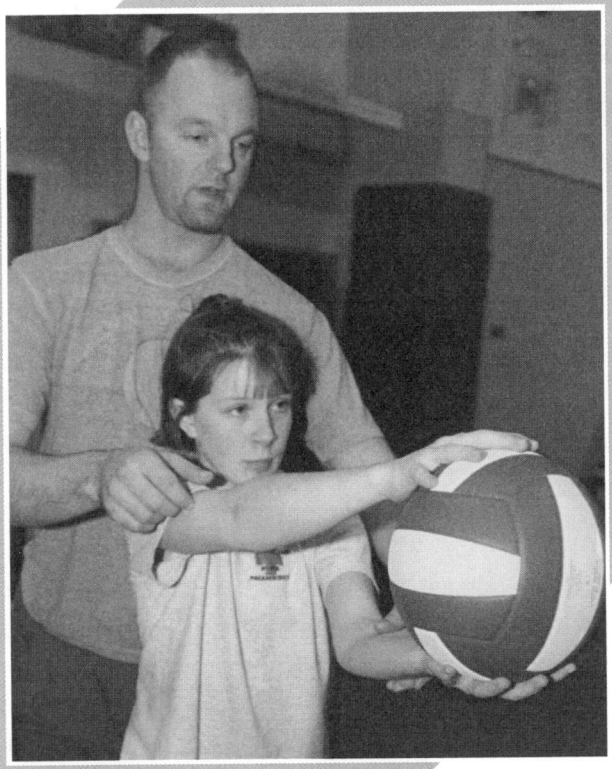

Teaching and Shaping Skills

Coaching volleyball is about teaching tactics, skills, fitness, values, and other useful things. It's also about coaching players before, during, and after contests. Teaching and coaching are closely related, but there are important differences. In this chapter we'll focus on principles of teaching, especially on teaching volleyball skills. But many of the principles we'll discuss apply to teaching tactics, fitness concepts, and values, all of which are elements of our curriculum. (Most of the other important teaching principles deal with communication, covered in chapter 2.) Then in chapter 6 we'll discuss the principles of coaching, which refer to your leadership activities during contests. Chapter 8 will address the teaching of tactics in a new way, using the games approach.

Teaching Volleyball Skills

Many people believe that the only qualification needed to teach a skill is to have performed it. It's helpful to have performed it, but there is much more than that to teaching successfully. And even if you haven't performed the skill before, you can still learn to teach successfully with the useful acronym IDEA:

I – Introduce the skill.
D – Demonstrate the skill.
E – Explain the skill.
A – Attend to players practicing the skill.

These are the basic steps of good teaching. Now we'll explain each step in greater detail.

Introduce the Skill

Players, especially young and inexperienced ones, need to know what skill they are learning and why they are learning it. You should therefore take these three steps every time you introduce a skill to your players:

1. Get your players' attention.
2. Name the skill.
3. Explain the importance of the skill.

Get Your Players' Attention

Because youngsters are easily distracted, use some method to get their attention. Some coaches use interesting news items or stories. Others use jokes. And still others simply project enthusiasm to get their players to listen. Whatever method you use, speak slightly above the normal volume and look your players in the eye when you speak.

Also, position players so they can see and hear you. Arrange the players in two or three evenly spaced rows, facing you. (Make sure there's no distracting activity behind you.) Then before you begin ask if all of them can see you.

Name the Skill

Although you might mention other common names for the skill, decide which one you'll use and stick with it. This will help avoid confusion and enhance communication among your players.

Explain the Importance of the Skill

Although the importance of a skill may be apparent to you, your players may be less able to see how the skill will help them become better volleyball players. Offer them a reason for learning the skill and describe how the skill relates to more advanced skills.

> *The most difficult aspect of coaching is this: Coaches must learn to let athletes learn. Sport skills should be taught so they have meaning to the child, not just meaning to the coach.*
>
> —Rainer Martens,
> founder of the American Sport Education Program

Demonstrate the Skill

The demonstration step is the most important part of teaching sport skills to players who may never have done anything closely resembling the skill. They need a picture, not just words. They need to see how the skill is performed.

If you are unable to perform the skill correctly, have an assistant coach, one of your players, or someone else more skilled perform the demonstration. These tips will help make your demonstrations more effective:

- Use correct form.
- Demonstrate the skill several times.
- Slow down the action, if possible, during one or two performances so players can see every movement involved in the skill.
- Perform the skill at different angles so your players can get a full perspective of it.
- Demonstrate the skill with both the right and the left hands.

Explain the Skill

Players learn more effectively when they're given a brief explanation of the skill along with the demonstration. Use simple terms and, if possible, relate the skill to previously learned skills. Ask your players whether they understand your description. A good technique is to ask the team to repeat your explanation. Ask questions like "What are you going to do first?" and "Then what?" Watch for when players look confused or uncertain, and repeat your explanation and demonstration at those points. If possible, use different words so your players get a chance to try to understand the skill from a different perspective.

Complex skills often are better understood when they are explained in more manageable parts. For instance, if you want to teach your players how to perform the crossover dribble, you might take the following steps:

1. Show them a correct performance of the entire skill and explain its function in volleyball.
2. Break down the skill and point out its component parts to your players.
3. Have players perform each of the component skills you have already taught them, such as beginning position, playing the ball from a low body position, and using a forearm platform to direct the ball to the target.
4. After players have demonstrated their ability to perform the separate parts of the skill in sequence, reexplain the entire skill.
5. Have players practice the skill in game-like conditions.

One caution: Young players have short attention spans, and a long demonstration or explanation of the skill will bore them. So spend no more than a few minutes altogether on the introduction, demonstration, and explanation phases. Then get the players active in a game that calls on them to perform the skill. The total IDEA should be completed in 10 minutes or less and followed by games in which players practice the skill.

Attend to Players Practicing the Skill

If the skill you selected was within your players' capabilities and you have done an effective job of introducing, demonstrating, and explaining it, your players should be ready to attempt the skill. Some players may need to be physically guided through the movements during their first few attempts. Walking unsure athletes through the skill in this way will help them gain confidence to perform the skill on their own.

Your teaching duties don't end when all your athletes have demonstrated that they understand how to perform the skill. In fact, a significant part of your teaching will involve observing closely the hit-and-miss trial performances of your players. In the next section we'll guide you in shaping players' skills, and then we'll help you learn how to detect and correct errors, using positive feedback. Keep in mind that your feedback will have a great influence on your players' motivation to practice and improve their performances.

Remember, too, that players need individual instruction. So set aside a time before, during, or after practice to give individual help.

Helping Players Improve Skills

After you have successfully taught your players the fundamentals of a skill, your focus will be on helping them improve that skill. Players will learn skills and improve upon them at different rates, so don't get too frustrated. Instead, help them improve by shaping their skills and detecting and correcting errors.

Shaping Players' Skills

One of your principal teaching duties is to reward positive behavior—in terms of successful skill execution—when you see it. A player makes a good pass in practice, and you immediately say, "Good pass! Way to use your fingers rather than your palms—and it was right on target." This plus a smile and a thumbs-up gesture goes a long way toward reinforcing that technique in that player.

However, sometimes you may have a long, dry spell before you have any correct technique to reinforce. It's difficult to reward players when they aren't executing skills correctly. How can you shape their skills if this is the case?

Shaping skills takes practice on your players' part and patience on your part. Expect your players to make errors. Telling the player who made the great pass that she did a good job doesn't ensure that she'll make that pass the next time. Seeing inconsistency in your players' techniques can be frustrating. It's even more challenging to stay positive when your athletes repeatedly perform a skill incorrectly or lack enthusiasm for learning. It can certainly be frustrating to see athletes who seemingly don't heed your advice and continue to make the same mistakes. And when the athletes don't seem to care, you may wonder why you should.

Please know that it is normal to get frustrated at times when teaching skills. Nevertheless, part of successful coaching is controlling this frustration. Instead of getting upset, use these six guidelines for shaping skills:

1. Think small initially. Reward the first signs of behavior that approximate what you want. Then reward closer and closer approximations of the desired behavior. In short, use your reward power to shape the behavior you seek.

2. Break skills into small steps. For instance, in learning to overhand serve, one of your players does well with her swing, but her toss is inconsistent. Reinforce the correct technique of her swing, and teach her how to make more consistent tosses. When she masters that, focus on getting her to serve to certain areas of the court.

3. Develop one component of a skill at a time. Don't try to shape two components of a skill at once. For example, in receiving serve, players must first move to the correct location, then set their position and execute the pass. They should focus first on one aspect (moving to the correct location) then on the others (setting their position and executing the pass). Athletes who have problems mastering a skill often do so because they're trying to improve two or more components at once. Help these athletes to isolate a single component.

4. As athletes become more proficient at a skill, reinforce them only occasionally and only for the best examples of the skill behavior. By focusing only on the best examples, you will help them continue to improve once they've mastered the basics.

5. When athletes are trying to master a new skill, temporarily relax your standards for how you reward them. As they focus on the new skill or attempt to integrate it with other skills, the old well-learned skills may temporarily degenerate.

6. If, however, a well-learned skill degenerates for long, you may need to restore it by going back to the basics.

Coaches often have more skilled players provide feedback to teammates as they practice skills. This can be effective, but proceed with caution: You must tell the skilled players exactly what to look for when their teammates are performing the skills. You must also tell them the corrections for the common errors of that skill.

Emphasize positive rather than negative errors. For example, a high set that is off target is better than a low set that is off target; the hitter had more of a change to recover. Serving or spiking over the net and out of bounds is better than serving or spiking into the net; an opponent might still play the ball.

We've looked at how to guide your athletes as they learn skills. Now let's look at another critical teaching principle that you should employ as you're shaping skills: detecting and correcting errors.

Detecting and Correcting Errors

Good coaches recognize that athletes make two types of errors: learning errors and performance errors. *Learning errors* are ones that occur because athletes don't know how to perform a skill; that is, they have not yet developed the correct motor program in the brain to perform a particular skill. *Performance errors* are made not because athletes don't know how to do the skill but because they made a mistake in executing what they do know. There is no easy way to know whether a player is making learning or performance errors. Part of the art of coaching is being able to sort out which type of error each mistake is.

The process of helping your athletes correct errors begins with your observing and evaluating their performances to determine if the mistakes are learning or performance errors. For performance errors, you need to look for the reasons that your athletes are not performing as well as they know how. If the mistakes are learning errors, then you need to help them learn the skill. That is the focus of this section.

There is no substitute for knowing skills well in correcting learning errors. The better you understand a skill—not only how it is done correctly but also what causes learning errors—the more helpful you will be in correcting mistakes.

One of the most common coaching mistakes is to provide inaccurate feedback and advice on how to correct errors. Don't rush into error correction; wrong feedback or poor advice will hurt the learning process more than no feedback or advice. If you are uncertain about the cause of the problem or how to correct it, continue to observe and analyze until you are more sure. As a rule, you should see the error repeated several times before attempting to correct it.

Correct One Error at a Time

Suppose Jill, one of your forwards, is having trouble with her spiking. She's doing most things well, but you notice that she's swinging her arms forward and up rather late as she approaches the ball, and she's contacting the ball behind her hitting shoulder, thus causing her spikes to sail high. What do you do?

First, decide which error to correct first because athletes learn more effectively when they attempt to correct one error at a time. Determine whether one error is causing the other; if so, have the athlete correct that error first because it may eliminate the other error. In Jill's case, raising her arms late may be causing her to contact the ball behind her hitting shoulder, so you should correct her late arm motion first. In cases where neither error is necessarily causing the other, correct the error that will bring the greatest improvement when remedied. Correcting one error often motivates athletes to correct other errors.

Use Positive Feedback to Correct Errors

The positive approach to correcting errors includes emphasizing what to do instead of what not to do. Use compliments, praise, rewards, and encouragement to correct errors. Acknowledge correct performance as well as efforts to improve. By using the positive approach, you can help your athletes feel good about themselves and promote a strong desire to achieve.

When you're working with one athlete at a time, the positive approach to correcting errors includes four steps:

1. Praise effort and correct performance.
2. Give simple and precise feedback to correct errors.
3. Make sure the athlete understands your feedback.
4. Provide an environment that motivates the athlete to improve.

Let's take a brief look at each step.

Step 1: Praise Effort and Correct Performance. Praise your athlete for trying to perform a skill correctly and for performing any parts of it correctly. Praise the athlete immediately after he or she performs the skill, if possible. Keep the praise simple: "Good try," "Way to hustle," "Good form," "Good extension," or "That's the way to follow through." You can also use nonverbal feedback, such as smiling, clapping your hands, or any facial or body expression that shows approval.

Make sure you're sincere with your praise. Don't indicate that an athlete's effort was good when it wasn't. Usually an athlete knows when he or she has made a sincere effort to perform the skill correctly and perceives undeserved praise for what it is—untruthful feedback to make him or her feel good. Likewise, don't indicate that a player's performance was correct when it wasn't.

Step 2: Give Simple and Precise Feedback. Don't burden a player with a long or detailed explanation of how to correct an error. Give just enough feedback so the player can correct one error at a time. Before giving feedback, recognize that some athletes will readily accept it immediately after the error; others will respond better if you slightly delay the correction.

For errors that are complicated to explain and difficult to correct, try the following:

- Explain and demonstrate what the athlete should have done. Do not demonstrate what the athlete did wrong.

- Explain the cause or causes of the error if this isn't obvious.
- Explain why you are recommending the correction you have selected if it's not obvious.

Step 3: Make Sure the Athlete Understands Your Feedback. If the athlete doesn't understand your feedback, he or she won't be able to correct the error. Ask him or her to repeat the feedback and to explain and demonstrate how it will be used. If the athlete can't do this, be patient and present your feedback again. Then have the athlete repeat the feedback after you're finished.

Step 4: Provide an Environment That Motivates the Athlete to Improve. Your players won't always be able to correct their errors immediately even if they do understand your feedback. Encourage them to "hang tough" and stick with it when corrections are difficult or they seem discouraged. For more difficult corrections, remind them that it will take time, and the improvement will happen only if they work at it. Look to encourage players with low self-confidence. Saying something like, "You were serving much better today; with practice, you'll be able to get some real movement on the ball and make it difficult to receive," can motivate a player to continue to refine his or her skills.

Some athletes need to be more motivated to improve. Others may be very self-motivated and need little help from you in this area at all; with them you can practically ignore Step 4 when correcting an error. While motivation comes from within, look to provide an environment of positive instruction and encouragement to help your athletes improve.

A final note on correcting errors: Team sports such as volleyball provide unique challenges in this endeavor. How do you provide individual feedback in a group setting using a positive approach? Instead of yelling across the court to correct an error (and embarrassing the player), substitute for the player who erred. Then make the correction on the sidelines. This type of feedback has three advantages:

- The player will be more receptive to the one-on-one feedback.
- The other players are still active, still practicing skills, and unable to hear your discussion.
- Because the rest of the team is still playing, you'll feel compelled to make your comments simple and concise—which, as we've said, is more helpful to the player.

This doesn't mean you can't use the team setting to give specific, positive feedback. You can do so to emphasize correct group and individual performances. Use this team feedback approach *only* for positive statements, though. Keep any negative feedback for individual discussions.

Developing Practice Plans

You will need to create practice plans for each season. Each practice plan should contain the following sections:

- Purpose
- Equipment
- Plan

Purpose sections focus on what you want to teach your players during each practice; they outline your main theme for each practice. The purpose should be drawn from your season plan (see chapter 9). Equipment sections note what you'll need to have on hand for that practice. Plan sections outline what you will do during each practice session. Each consists of these elements:

- Warm-Up
- Games
- Skill Practices
- Cool-Down and Review
- Progressions

You'll begin each session with about five minutes of warm-up activities. Then you'll have your players play a modified volleyball game (look in chapter 8 for suggested games). You'll look for your cue to interrupt that game—your cue being when players are having problems with carrying out the basic goal or aim of the game. At this point you'll "freeze" the action, keeping the players where they are, and ask brief questions about the tactical problems the players encountered and what skills they need to solve those problems. (Review chapter 4 for more on interrupting a game and holding a question-and-answer session.)

Then you'll teach the skill the players need to acquire to successfully execute the tactic. During Skill Practice you'll use the IDEA approach:

- Introduce the skill.
- Demonstrate the skill.
- Explain the skill.
- Attend to players' practicing the skill.

Your introduction, demonstration, and explanation of a skill should take no more than two to three minutes; then you'll attend to players and provide teaching cues or further demonstration as necessary as they practice the skill.

After the Skill Practices, you will usually have the athletes play another game or two to let them use the skills they have just learned and to understand them in the context of a game. During Game and Skill Practices, emphasize the importance of every player on the court moving and being involved in every play, whether they will be directly touching the ball or not. No player on the court should be standing around.

The Plan section continues with a cool down and stretch. Following this you'll wrap up the practice with a few summary comments and remind them of the next practice or game day.

The games in chapter 8 include suggestions to help you modify the games. These suggestions will help you keep practices fun and provide activities for players with varying skill levels.

Although practicing using the games approach should reduce the need for discipline, there will be times when you'll have to deal with players who are misbehaving in practice. In the next section, we'll help you handle these situations.

Dealing With Misbehavior

Athletes will misbehave at times; it's only natural. Following are two ways you can respond to misbehavior: through extinction or discipline.

Extinction

Ignoring a misbehavior—neither rewarding nor disciplining it—is called *extinction*. This can be effective under certain circumstances. In some situations, disciplining young people's misbehavior only encourages them to act up further because of the recognition they get. Ignoring misbehavior teaches youngsters that it is not worth your attention.

Sometimes, though, you cannot wait for a behavior to fizzle out. When players cause danger to themselves or others or disrupt the activities of others, you need to take immediate action. Tell the offending player that the behavior must stop and that discipline will follow if it doesn't. If the athlete doesn't stop misbehaving after the warning, discipline.

Extinction also doesn't work well when a misbehavior is self-rewarding. For example, you may be able to keep from grimacing if a youngster kicks you in the shin, but he or she still knows you were hurt. Therein lies the reward. In these circumstances, it is also necessary to discipline the player for the undesirable behavior.

Extinction works best in situations in which players are seeking recognition through mischievous behaviors, clowning, or grandstanding. Usually, if you are patient, their failure to get your attention will cause the behavior to disappear.

However, be alert that you don't extinguish desirable behavior. When youngsters do something well, they expect to be positively reinforced. Not rewarding them will likely cause them to discontinue the desired behavior.

Discipline

Some educators say we should never discipline young people but should only reinforce their positive behaviors. They argue that discipline does not work, it creates hostility, and sometimes develops avoidance behaviors that may be more unwholesome than the original problem behavior. It is true that discipline does not always work and that it can create problems when used ineffectively, but when used appropriately, discipline is effective in eliminating undesirable behaviors without creating other undesirable consequences. You must use discipline effectively because it is impossible to guide athletes through positive reinforcement and extinction alone. Discipline is part of the positive approach when these guidelines are followed:

- Discipline in a corrective way to help athletes improve now and in the future. Don't discipline to retaliate and make yourself feel better.
- Impose discipline in an impersonal way when athletes break team rules or otherwise misbehave. Shouting at or scolding athletes indicates that your attitude is one of revenge.
- Once a good rule has been agreed upon, ensure that athletes who violate it experience the unpleasant consequences of their misbehavior. Don't wave discipline threateningly over their heads. Just do it, but warn an athlete once before disciplining.
- Be consistent in administering discipline.
- Don't discipline using consequences that may cause you guilt. If you can't think of an appropriate consequence right away, tell the player you will talk with him or her after you think about it. You might consider involving the player in designing a consequence.
- Once the discipline is completed, don't make athletes feel they are "in the doghouse." Make them feel that they're valued members of the team.
- Make sure that what you think is discipline isn't perceived by the athlete as a positive reinforcement—for instance, keeping a player

out of doing a certain drill or portion of the practice may be just what the athlete desired.

- Never discipline athletes for making errors when they are playing.
- Never use physical activity—running laps or doing push-ups—as discipline. To do so only causes athletes to resent physical activity, something we want them to learn to enjoy throughout their lives.
- Discipline sparingly. Constant discipline and criticism cause athletes to turn their interests elsewhere and to resent you as well.

chapter 6

Game-Day Coaching

Contests provide the opportunity for your players to show what they've learned in practice. Just as your players' focuses shift on contest days from learning and practicing to *competing,* so your focus shifts from teaching skills to coaching players as they perform those skills in contests. Of course, the contest is a teaching opportunity as well, but the focus is on performing what has been previously learned.

In the last chapter you learned how to teach your players volleyball tactics and skills; in this chapter we'll help you coach your players as they execute those tactics and skills in contests. We'll provide important coaching principles that will guide you throughout the game day—before, during, and after the contest.

Before the Contest

Just as you need a practice plan for what you're going to do each practice, you need a game plan for what to do on the day of a game. Many inexperienced coaches focus only on how they will coach during the contest itself, but your preparations to coach should include details that begin well before the first play of the game. In fact, your preparations should begin during the practice before the contest.

Preparations at Practice

During the practice a day or two before the next contest, you should do two things (besides practicing tactics and skills) to prepare your players: Decide on any specific team tactics that you want to employ, and discuss pregame particulars, such as what to eat before the game, what to wear, and when to be at the court.

Deciding Team Tactics

Some coaches see themselves as great military strategists guiding their young warriors to victory on the battlefield. These coaches burn the midnight oil as they devise a complex plan of attack. There are several things wrong with this approach, but we'll point out two errors in terms of deciding team tactics:

1. The decision on team tactics should be made with input from players.
2. Team tactics at this level don't need to be complex.

Perhaps you guessed right on the second point but were surprised by the first. Why should you include your players in deciding tactics? Isn't that the coach's role?

It's the coach's role to help youngsters grow through the sport experience. Allowing your athletes input here helps them to learn the game. It gets them involved at a planning level that often is reserved solely for the coach. It gives them a feeling of ownership; they're not just "carrying out orders" of the coach. They're executing the plan of attack that was jointly decided. Youngsters who have a say in how they approach a task often respond with more enthusiasm and motivation.

Don't dampen that enthusiasm and motivation by concocting tactics that are too complex. Keep tactics simple, especially at the younger levels. Focus on simple offensive alignments, on proper positioning and court coverage, and on setting up good attacks.

As you become more familiar with your team's tendencies and abilities, help them focus on specific tactics that will help them play better. For example, if your team has a tendency to stand around and watch the action, emphasize moving more and spreading out the attack. If they are active and moving throughout the game but not in any cohesive fashion, focus them on communicating on the court, calling the ball, and being ready to play an errant pass.

If you're coaching 12- to 14-year-olds, you might institute certain plays that your team has practiced. These plays should take advantage of your players' strengths. Again, give the players some input into what plays might be employed in a game.

Discussing Precontest Particulars

Players need to know what to do before a contest: what they should eat on game day and when, what clothing they should wear to the game, what equipment they should bring, and what time they should arrive at the court. Discuss these particulars with them at the practice before a contest. Here are guidelines for discussing these issues.

Pregame Meal. Carbohydrates are easily digested and absorbed and are a ready source of fuel. Players should eat a high-carbohydrate meal ideally about three to four hours before a game to allow the stomach to empty completely. This won't be possible for games held in early morning; in this case, athletes should still eat food high in carbohydrates, such as an English muffin, toast, or cereal, but not so much that their stomachs are full. In addition, athletes' pregame meals shouldn't include foods that are spicy or high in fat content.

Clothing and Equipment. Instruct players to wear their team shirts or uniforms, shorts, suitable shoes, and sweats.

Time to Arrive. Your players will need to adequately warm up before a game, so instruct them to arrive 20 minutes before a game to go through a team warm-up (see "The Warm-Up" later in this chapter).

Facilities, Equipment, and Support Personnel

Although the site coordinator and officials have responsibilities regarding facilities and equipment, it's wise for you to know what to look for to make sure the contest is safe for the athletes. You should arrive at the court 25 to 30 minutes before game time so you can check the court, check in with the site coordinator and officials, and greet your players as they arrive to warm up. The site coordinator and officials should be checking the facilities and preparing for the contest. If officials aren't arriving before the game when they're supposed to, inform the site coordinator. A facilities checklist includes the following:

Gymnasium Facilities

- ✔ The stairs and corridors leading to the gym are well lit.
- ✔ The stairs and corridors are free of obstruction.
- ✔ The stairs and corridors are in good repair.
- ✔ Exits are well marked and illuminated.
- ✔ Exits are free of obstruction.
- ✔ Uprights and other projections are padded.
- ✔ Walls are free of projections.
- ✔ Windows are located high on the walls.
- ✔ Wall plugs and light switches are insulated and protected.
- ✔ Lights are shielded.
- ✔ Lighting is sufficient to illuminate the playing area well.
- ✔ The heating/cooling system for the gym is working properly and is monitored regularly.
- ✔ Ducts, radiators, pipes, and so on are shielded or designed to withstand high impact.
- ✔ Tamper-free thermostats are housed in impact-resistant covers.
- ✔ The track has secure railings with a minimum height of three feet, six inches.
- ✔ The track has direction signs posted.
- ✔ The track is free of obstructions.
- ✔ Rules for the track are posted.
- ✔ Projections on the track are padded or illuminated.
- ✔ Gym equipment is inspected prior to and during each use.
- ✔ The gym is adequately supervised.
- ✔ Galleries and viewing areas have been designed to protect small children by blocking their access to the playing area.
- ✔ The gym (floor, roof, walls, light fixtures, etc.) is inspected on an annual basis for safety and structural deficiencies.
- ✔ Fire alarms are in good working order.
- ✔ Fire extinguishers are up to date, with note of last inspection.
- ✔ Directions are posted for evacuating the gym in case of fire.

Communicating With Parents

The groundwork for your communication with parents will have been laid in the parent orientation program, through which parents learn the best ways to support their kids'—and the whole team's—efforts on the court. As parents gather in the gym before a contest, let them know what the team has been focusing on during the past week and what your goals are for the game. For instance, perhaps you've worked on transitioning to attack in practice this week; encourage parents to watch for improvement and success in executing this tactic and to support the team members as they attempt all tactics and skills. Help parents to judge success not just based on the contest outcome but on how the kids are improving their performances.

If parents yell at the kids for mistakes made during the game, make disparaging remarks about the officials or opponents, or shout instructions on what tactics to employ, ask them to refrain from making such remarks and to instead be supportive of the team in their comments and actions.

After a contest, briefly and informally assess with parents, as the opportunity arises, how the team did based not on the outcome but on meeting performance goals and playing to the best of their abilities. Help parents see the contest as a process not solely as a test that's pass/fail or win/lose. Encourage parents to reinforce that concept at home.

Unplanned Events

Part of being prepared to coach is to expect the unexpected. What do you do if players are late? What if *you* have an emergency and can't make the game or will be late? What if the contest is postponed? Being prepared to handle out-of-the-ordinary circumstances will help you when such unplanned events happen.

If players are late, you may have to adjust your starting lineup. While this may not be a major inconvenience, do stress to your players the importance of being on time for two reasons:

- Part of being a member of a team means being committed and responsible to the other members. When players don't show up or show up late, they break that commitment.
- Players need to go through a warm-up to physically prepare for the contest. Skipping the warm-up risks injury.

Consider making a team rule stating that players need to show up 20 minutes before a game and go through the complete team warm-up, or they won't start.

An emergency might cause *you* to be late or miss a game. In such cases, notify your assistant coach, if you have one, or the league coordinator. If notified in advance, a parent of a player or another volunteer might be able to step in for the contest.

Sometimes a game will be postponed because of inclement weather or for other reasons (such as unsafe court conditions). If the postponement takes place before game day, you'll need to call each member of your team to let him or her know. If it happens while the teams are on the court preparing for the game, gather your team members and tell them the news and why the game is being postponed. Make sure all your players have rides home before you leave—be the last to leave to be sure.

The Warm-Up

Players need to both physically and mentally prepare for a game once they arrive at the court. Physical preparation involves warming up. We've suggested that players arrive 20 minutes before the game to warm up. Conduct the warm-up similar to practice warm-ups, with some brief games that focus on skill practice and stretching.

Players should prepare to do what they will do in the game: serve, receive serve, overhead pass, forearm pass, spike, dig, and so on. This doesn't mean they spend extensive time on each skill; you can plan two or three brief practice games that encompass all these skills.

After playing a few brief games, your players should stretch. You don't need to deliver any big pep talk, but you can help your players mentally prepare as they stretch by reminding them of the following:

- The tactics and skills they've been working on in recent practices, especially focusing their attention on what they've been doing well. Focus on their strengths.
- The team tactics you decided on in your previous practice.
- Performing the tactics and skills to the best of their individual abilities and playing together as a team.
- Playing hard and smart and having fun!

During the Contest

The list you just read goes a long way toward defining your focus for coaching during the contest. Throughout the game, you'll keep the game in proper perspective and help your players do the same. You'll observe how your players execute tactics and skills and how well they play together. You'll make tactical decisions in a number of areas. You'll model appropriate behavior on the bench, showing respect for opponents and officials, and demand the same of your athletes. You'll watch out for your athletes' physical safety and psychological welfare, in terms of building their self-esteem and helping them manage stress and anxiety.

Proper Perspective

Winning games is the short-term goal of your volleyball program; helping your players learn the tactics, skills, and rules of volleyball, how to become fit, and how to be good sports in volleyball and in life is the long-term goal. Your young athletes are "winning" when they are becoming better human beings through their participation in volleyball. Keep that perspective in mind when you coach. *You* have the privilege of setting the tone for how your team approaches the game. Keep winning and all aspects of the competition in proper perspective, and your young charges will likely follow suit.

Tactical Decisions

While you aren't called upon to be a great military strategist, you are called upon to make tactical decisions in several areas throughout a contest. You'll make decisions about who starts the game and when to enter substitutes, about making slight adjustments to your team's tactics, and about correcting players' performance errors or leaving the correction for the next practice.

Starting and Substituting Players

In considering playing time, make sure that everyone plays at least half of each game. This should be your guiding principle as you consider starting and substitution patterns.

Adjusting Team Tactics

At the 8 to 9 and 10 to 11 age levels, you probably won't adjust your team tactics too significantly during a game; rather, you'll focus on the basic tactics in general and emphasize during breaks which tactics your team needs to work on in particular. However, coaches of 12- to 14-year-olds might have cause to make tactical adjustments to improve their team's chances of performing well and winning. As games progress, assess your opponents' style of play and tactics, and make adjustments that are appropriate—that is, that your players are prepared for.

However, don't stress tactics too much during a game. Doing so can take the fun out of the game for the players. If you don't trust your memory, carry a pen and notepad to note which team tactics and individual skills need attention in the next practice.

Correcting Players' Errors

In chapter 5 you learned about two types of errors: learning errors and performance errors. Learning errors are ones that occur because athletes don't know how to perform a skill. Athletes make performance errors not because they don't know how to do the skill, but because they make a mistake in executing what they do know.

Sometimes it's not easy to tell which type of error athletes are making. Knowing your athletes' capabilities helps you to know whether they know the skill and are simply making mistakes in executing it or whether they don't really know how to perform the skill. If they are making learning errors—that is, they don't know how to perform the skills—you'll need to make note of this and teach them at the next practice. Game time is not the time to teach skills.

If they are making performance errors, however, you can help players correct those errors during a game. Players who make performance errors often do so because they have a lapse in concentration or motivation—or they are simply demonstrating the human quality of sometimes doing things incorrectly. A word of encouragement to concentrate more may help. If you do correct a performance error during a contest, do so in a quiet, controlled, and positive tone of voice during a break or when the player is on the bench with you.

For those making performance errors, you have to decide if it is just the occasional error anyone makes or an expected error for a youngster at that stage of development. If that is the case, then the player may appreciate your not commenting on the mistake. The player knows it was a mistake and knows how to correct it. On the other hand, perhaps an encouraging word and a "coaching cue" (such as "Remember to tilt your forearm platform to direct the ball to your target") may be just what the athlete needs. Knowing the players and what to say is very much a part of the "art" of coaching.

Coach's and Players' Behavior

Another aspect of coaching on game day is managing behavior—both yours and your athletes'. The two are closely connected.

Your Conduct

You very much influence your players' behavior before, during, and after a contest. If you're up, your players are more likely to be up. If you're anxious, they'll notice and the anxiety can be contagious. If you're negative, they'll respond with worry. If you're positive, they'll play with more enjoyment. If you're constantly yelling instructions or commenting on mistakes and errors, it will be difficult for players to concentrate. Instead, let players get into the flow of the game.

The focus should be on positive competition and on having fun. A coach who overorganizes everything and dominates a game from the sideline is definitely *not* making the contest fun.

So how should you conduct yourself on the bench? Here are a few pointers:

- Be calm, in control, and supportive of your players.
- Encourage players often, but instruct during play sparingly. Players should be focusing on their performance during a game, not on instructions shouted from the bench.
- If you need to instruct a player, do so when you're both on the bench, in an unobtrusive manner. Never yell at players for making a mistake. Instead, briefly demonstrate or remind them of the correct technique and encourage them.

Remember, you're not playing for an Olympic gold medal! In this program, volleyball competitions are designed to help players develop their skills and themselves—and to have fun. So coach in a manner at games that helps your players do those things.

Players' Conduct

You're responsible for keeping your players under control. Do so by setting a good example and by disciplining when necessary. Set team rules of good behavior. If players attempt to cheat, fight, argue, badger, yell disparaging remarks, and the like, it is your responsibility to correct the misbehavior. Consider team rules in these areas of game conduct:

- Players' language
- Players' behavior
- Interactions with officials
- Discipline for misbehavior
- Dress code for competitions

Players' Physical Safety

We devoted all of chapter 3 to discussing how to provide for players' safety, but it's worth noting here that safety during contests can be affected by how officials are calling the rules. If they aren't calling rules correctly, and this risks injury to your players, you must intervene. Voice your concern in a respectful manner and in a way that places the emphasis where it should be: on the athletes' safety. One of the officials' main responsibilities is to provide for athletes' safety; you are not adversaries here. Don't hesitate to address an issue of safety with an official when the need arises.

Players' Psychological Welfare

Athletes often attach their self-worth to winning and losing. This idea is fueled by coaches, parents, peers, and society, who place great emphasis on winning. Players become anxious when they're uncertain if they can meet the expectations of others or of themselves when meeting these expectations is important to them.

If you place too much importance on the game or cause your athletes to doubt their abilities, they will become anxious about the outcome and their performance. If your players look uptight and anxious during a contest, find ways to reduce both the uncertainties about how their performance will be evaluated and the importance they are attaching to the game. Help athletes focus on realistic personal goals—goals that are reachable and measurable and that will help them improve their performance. Another way to reduce anxiety on game day is to stay away from emotional pregame pep talks. We provided guidance earlier in what to address before the game.

When coaching during contests, remember that the most important outcome from playing volleyball is to build or enhance players' self-worth. Keep that firmly in mind, and strive to make every coaching decision promote your athletes' self-worth.

Opponents and Officials

Respect opponents and officials. Without them, you wouldn't have a competition. Officials help provide a fair and safe experience for athletes and, as appropriate, help them learn the game. Opponents provide opportunities for your team to test itself, improve, and excel.

You and your team should show respect for opponents by giving your best efforts. You owe them this. Showing respect doesn't necessarily mean being "nice" to your opponents, though it does mean being civil.

Don't allow your players to "trash talk" or taunt an opponent. Such behavior is disrespectful to the spirit of the competition and to the opponent. Immediately remove a player from a contest if he or she disobeys your orders in this area.

Remember that officials are quite often teenagers—in many cases not much older than the players themselves. The level of officiating should be commensurate to the level of play. In other words, don't expect perfection from officials any more than you do from your own players. And realize that the officials are there to help players learn the rules and skills, too.

After the Contest

When the game is over, join your team in congratulating the coaches and players of the opposing team, then be sure to thank the officials. Check on any injuries players sustained and let players know how to care for them. Be prepared to speak with the officials about any problems that occurred during the game. Then hold a brief Team Circle, as explained in a moment, to ensure your players are on an even keel, whether they won or lost.

Winning With Class, Losing With Dignity

When celebrating a victory, make sure your team does so in a way that doesn't show disrespect for the opponents. It's fine and appropriate to be happy and celebrate a win, but don't allow your players to taunt the opponents or boast about their victory. Keep winning in perspective. Winning and losing are a part of life, not just a part of sport. If players can handle both equally well, they'll be successful in whatever they do.

Athletes are competitors, and competitors will be disappointed in defeat. If your team has made a winning effort, let them know that. After a loss, help them keep their chins up and maintain a positive attitude that will carry over into the next practice and contest.

Team Circle

If your players have performed well in a game, compliment them and congratulate them immediately afterward. Tell them specifically what they did well, whether they won or lost. This will reinforce their desire to repeat their good performances.

Don't criticize individual players for poor performances in front of teammates. Help players improve their skills, but do so in the next practice, not immediately after a game.

The postgame Team Circle isn't the time to go over tactical problems and adjustments. The players are either so happy after a win or so dejected after a loss that they won't absorb much tactical information immediately following a game. Your first concern should be your players' attitudes and mental well-being. You don't want them to be too high after a win or too low after a loss. This is the time you can be most influential in keeping the outcome in perspective and keeping them on an even keel.

Finally, make sure your players have transportation home. Be the last one to leave in order to help if transportation falls through and to ensure full supervision of players before they leave.

chapter 7

Rules and Equipment

This is where we'll introduce you to some of the basic rules and traditions of volleyball. We won't try to cover all the rules of the game, but rather will give you what you need to work with players who are 8 to 14 years old. We'll give you information on equipment, court size and markings, player positions, scoring, and game play. We'll also recommend rules modifications to make the sport more appropriate for youngsters. In a short section at the end of the chapter we'll show you the officiating signals for volleyball.

Court

All lines marking the playing area on hard courts are two inches wide. Sporting goods stores and volleyball supply companies carry plastic tape especially made for marking volleyball courts on gym floors. Court markings on grass and beach surfaces usually are made of rope, which marks the perimeter of the court. The ropes are secured with stakes or other similar items that delineate the court while also maintaining the safety of the environment for the participants. Ensure that the stakes you use can be placed in the ground without potentially tripping an athlete, which could lead to serious injury; follow the manufacturer's instructions! Balls landing on the lines are inbounds in volleyball, so when marking court dimensions, measure from the outside of the lines. Note that players may go off the court to play a ball. A ball coming from the opponent that appears to be going out of bounds may not be caught or picked up until it legally touches an out-of-bounds area.

Usually, for playing games up through 4 v 4, you do not use the attack line because all the players, whether in the front court or backcourt, can attack the ball (see figure 7.1). If your team is playing 6 v 6, however, it would use the attack line. Place the marking about 10 feet from the net on each side of the court. It is not common to use the attack line on grass or beach surfaces.

Note that while we recommend specific court sizes in figure 7.1, you should adjust your court size and equipment to meet the needs of your program. Create what you need to make your program successful. For instance, use tennis, racquetball, or squash courts or play on grass, sand, concrete, or asphalt. Put one 10-meter-long adult net to use on *two* kids' courts, with a 2-meter buffer in between. Or use rope nets with flags or markers down to separate the court areas. It's not necessary to anchor the bottom of the net. You can also use badminton nets.

Ball

Table 7.1 shows our recommendations for using lighter and softer balls for players. To teach skills and vary the learning environment, you can even use punch balloons, beach balls, or rubber-bladder balls with durable, thin-foam coatings. All these balls are widely available from volleyball outlets.

Ideally, each player should have his or her own volleyball to make it easy to practice at home. This gives players a chance to become more familiar with the weight and feel of the ball.

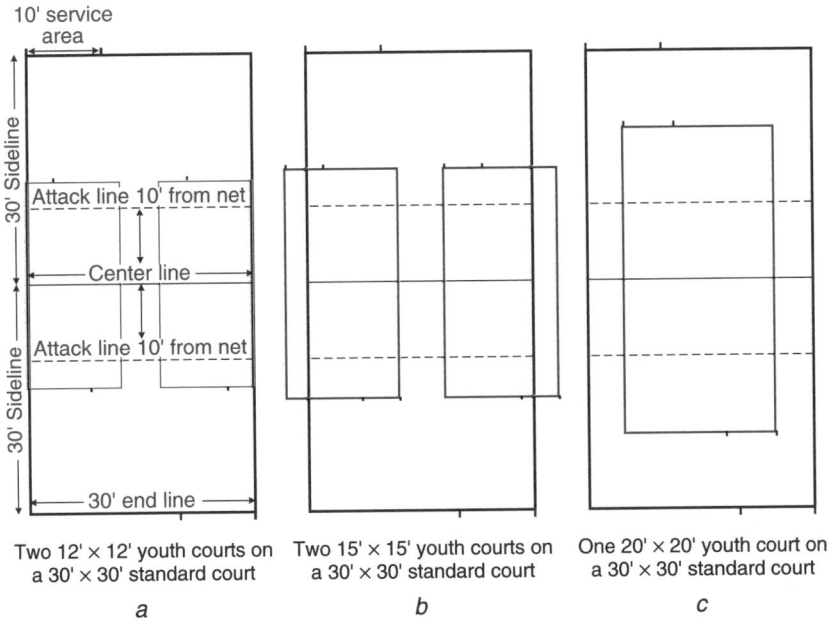

Figure 7.1 Three modifications of the standard court for youth volleyball.

Table 7.1 Rule Modifications for Volleyball

Item	8- to 9-year-olds	10- to 11-year-olds	12- to 14-year-olds
Players on team	8 (4)	10 (5)	9
Players on court	3 v 3	4 v 4	6 v 6
Ball	Beach balls, "gator" balls, or light (#5)	Oversized (#6) or light (#5)	Oversized (#6) or light (#5)
Court size	20' x 20'	20' x 20'	30' x 30'
Net height	6'	6'6"	7' to 7'4 1/8"
Length of contest	Games to 25, 25, and 15; best of 3 games	Games to 25, 25, and 15; best of 3 games	Games to 25, 25, and 15; best of 3 games
Scoring system	Rally	Rally	Rally

Players

Next we'll look at rules for players' equipment and provide guidelines for players' positions in various alignments. We'll also look at player rotation rules and substitution methods.

Equipment

Individual player equipment is inexpensive and, like volleyballs, fairly easy to obtain. Here's a list of what your players will need.

⊙ **Uniforms.** Uniforms can be as simple as shorts and a T-shirt or a long-sleeved shirt. Some players like the protection of long sleeves. Although warmer, these sleeves ease the sting of the ball on the forearms. In beach volleyball, uniforms vary more widely. Swimsuits or athletic shorts and a short-sleeved or sleeveless shirt are appropriate. For playing outside, consider the weather conditions as you choose appropriate clothing.

⊙ **Shoes.** A good shoe supports the arch and cushions the heel and ball of the foot. Volleyball or court shoes are fine for playing on hard courts. Running shoes aren't good, however, because they don't give lateral support. Volleyball shoes should be comfortable and broken in before they're worn during intense activity. Some players choose to wear shoes on grassy surfaces, while others prefer to play barefoot on the grass. Most beach players go barefoot or play with protective socks to avoid heat exposure or burning from the sand.

⊙ **Knee pads.** Knee pads are typically worn for games played on hard surfaces. The use of knee pads on the beach and grass is not prohibited, but it's not as popular as on harder surfaces. Knee pads come in a variety of shapes and sizes; most of them are made of foam or rubber covered with a soft elastic material. The pads should fit snugly and be comfortable for long periods. Because knee pads are designed to protect the knees, they make it a lot easier for young athletes to tolerate hitting the floor. If your local sporting goods store doesn't carry knee pads, you can order them through volleyball magazines or catalogs.

Positions

The basic concepts of three-, four- and six-a-side games are similar, so we'll present information only about player responsibilities in three-player and six-player games. You can easily adapt the material for four-a-side games. Before explaining player positions, however, we want to emphasize the important role you play in helping your athletes learn *all* the positions.

Beginners should work on developing all the basic skills of volleyball without specializing in any one position. Many times, due to differences in physical, mental, or social maturity, young players are pushed into specialized roles (the tallest players are taught only to block and hit; the shortest players are expected only to pass and set) only to later find that other roles are more appropriate for them. All players must develop the fundamental skills of volleyball (serving, passing, setting, hitting, individual defense, and blocking) to play the game effectively. Give your players the opportunity to enhance their skills in competition and their lifetime enjoyment of the sport by assuring they each play all the positions.

Three-Player Positions

In three-a-side volleyball, the players position themselves so that one player is in the front half of the court (front court) and the other two players split the back half (backcourt). Figure 7.2 shows the basic serve-receive positions used to start a 3 v 3 game.

Player A. Player A becomes a defensive player after initiating the serve. Player A is also one of the serve-receivers in the back row. This player will become the secondary setter if player B (the primary setter) receives the first ball over the net. Player A is in the first contact position (see figure 7.3).

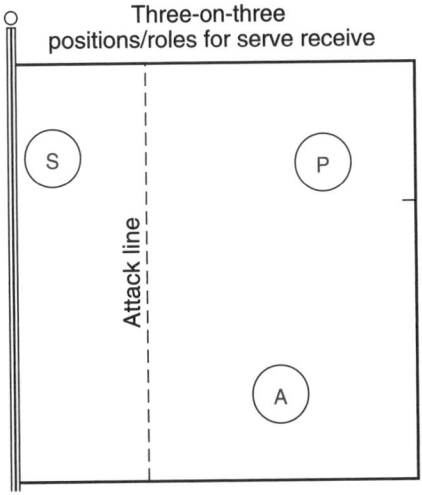

Figure 7.2 Serve-receive positions for 3 v 3 volleyball.

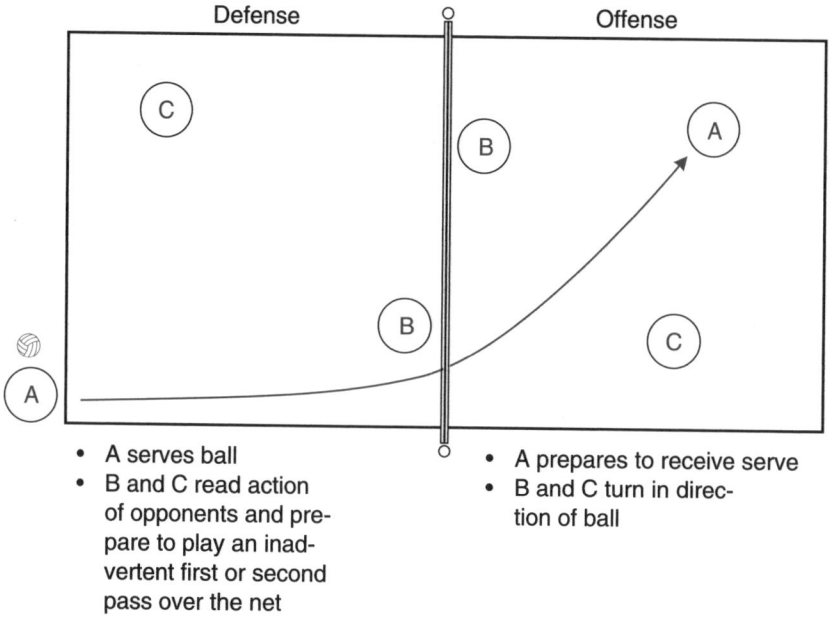

Figure 7.3 Primary responsibilities of Player A.

Player B. Player B is the primary setter on offense and the primary blocker on defense. This player becomes the secondary attacker if player C (the primary attacker) makes the second contact and must set for player B. However, player B should always strive to make the second contact (see figure 7.4).

Player C. Player C is the primary attacker on offense and primary digger on defense. This player will be the secondary digger or secondary setter if the served or attacked ball goes to player A or B. Player C will take most of the third contacts (see figure 7.5).

Six-Player Positions

In six-a-side volleyball, players are positioned similarly to three-a-side to cover the front court and backcourt areas. Figure 7.6 shows the basic serve-receive positions used to start a game in six-on-six volleyball.

In the six-player formation each player has specific responsibilities. Their roles and primary responsibilities are described here.

Right-Back and Left-Back Players. The right-back and left-back players will have primary serve-receive responsibility. Following serve reception, these players become concerned with covering any ball that might be blocked by the opponent. Assuming the ball crosses the net into the

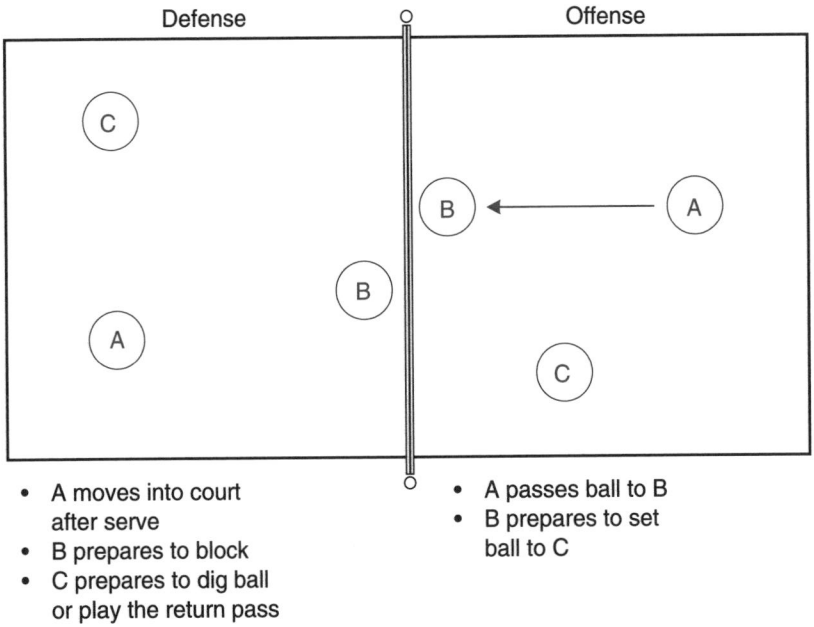

Figure 7.4 Primary responsibilities of Player B.

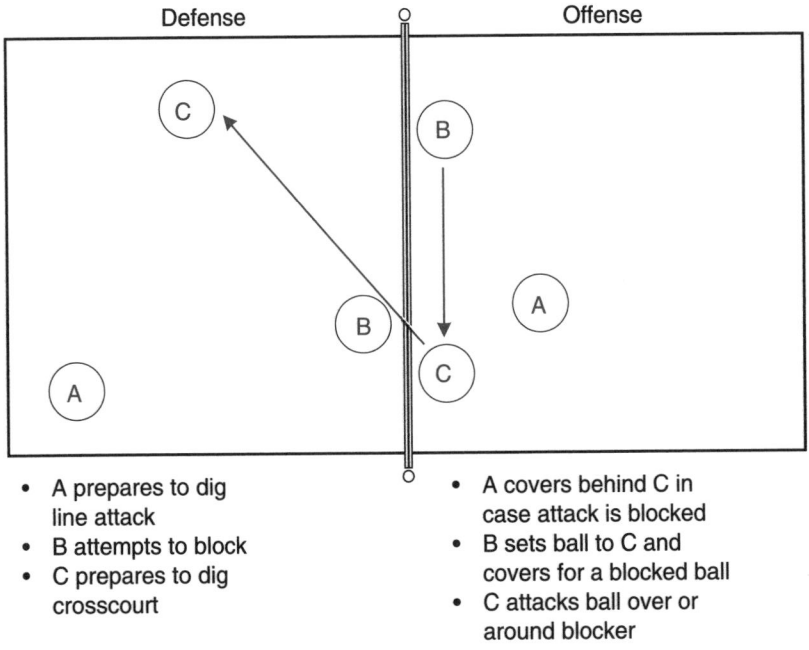

Figure 7.5 Primary responsibilities of Player C.

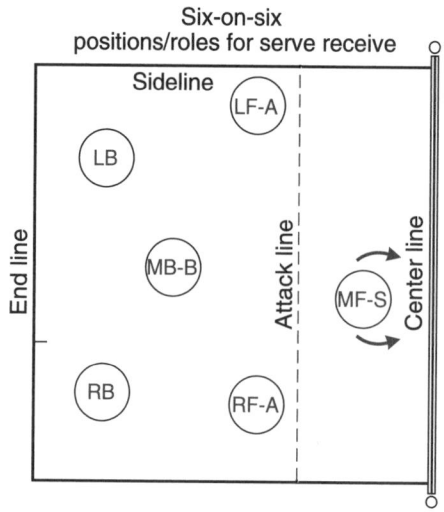

Figure 7.6 Serve-receive positions for 6 v 6 volleyball.

opponent's court and is kept in play by the opponent, they become defensive players.

Middle-Back Player. The middle-back player will have primary defensive responsibility but not primary serve-reception responsibility. Once again, you may modify serve-reception patterns, if you wish, to include the middle-back player in the serve-reception lineup.

Left-Front and Right-Front Players. The left-front and right-front players will be both the primary attackers on offense and important blockers on defense. They will be responsible for attacking the sets given by the setter and blocking attacks from the opponents. They will have very little responsibility in serve reception, unless you choose to modify serve-reception patterns to give them more responsibility.

Middle-Front Player. The middle-front player has primary responsibility for setting the second ball, allowing for an attack. The middle-front player will primarily set to the left-front and right-front players. If the middle-front player is unable to set the ball due to an errant pass, he or she is responsible for calling for help so that another player still can give a set.

Note: The right-back, left-back, and middle-back players are also called *back-row players;* the left-front, right-front, and middle-front players are also called *front-row players.*

As players develop their skills, they'll become comfortable playing anywhere on the court. Try to be patient and supportive as your players learn the skills they need to play successfully in all positions. Young players need a solid base to gain confidence and enthusiasm for playing volleyball. As their coach, help them learn the skills and positions well. They'll be glad you did.

Player Rotation

The lineup at the beginning of the game determines the service order throughout the game. Players of both teams must be in their correct rotational order at the time of the service by either team. The correct position of each player is described as follows:

- In the front line, the middle-front player must be between the right-front and left-front players and in front of the middle-back player.
- In the back line, the middle-back player must be between the right-back and left-back players and behind the middle-front player.
- The right-front player must be in front of the right-back player, and the left-front player must be in front of the left-back player.

When a player is out of position, play is stopped, the error is corrected, points scored while the team was in error are canceled, and a point is awarded to the opponent. After the serve, players may move to any court position they wish. Players rotate one position clockwise when their team obtains the serve.

Substitutions

Every player must play at least half of each competition. Various ways to substitute allow the players plenty of chances to improve their skills. The most common method is to allow a team member who is out to replace the person who has just rotated back to serve. This makes sense: the players understand when and whom to substitute, or go in, for. It virtually assures everyone equal playing time.

Another substitution method is to pair people in each position (two players are assigned to right-back, two to left-back, and so on) and split the game in half. If you're playing to 15 points, players come in to substitute for the partner when one team has reached 8 points. Remember to give each player the opportunity to start the game and to come in at the halfway point, so you ensure equal repetitions. Remember, although winning is fun both for you and your athletes, it should take a back seat to everyone's having the chance to practice and play the game.

For 2001, USA Volleyball has created a new rule that allows one designated player, called a *libero,* unlimited substitution into the back row. For more information about this new position and how a libero may be used in a game, check the current edition of the rulebook.

In the six-a-side game, each team is allowed two time-outs per game. Time-outs last 30 seconds. While the substitution rules with the *traditional* six-player team games are relatively strict, be willing to modify these rules to ensure each player gets the opportunity to participate. You might have unlimited team substitutions for a team or individual, or you might substitute for the player who is getting ready to serve, regardless of who that person is.

Scoring

Various scoring methods are used in volleyball. In all these scoring methods, the team that commits an error (hitting the ball out of bounds, into the net, and so on) forfeits its opportunity to serve:

- **Rally scoring.** A point is scored on every serve, no matter which team served. The team who wins the point gets to serve the next point. For example, team A serves the ball out of bounds, so team B gets the point and the next serve. This is the only format in which the nonserving team can score points.
- **Side-out scoring.** Games are played to 15 points, one point at a time. Only the serving team may score points, and a team must win by 2 points. A *match* consists of one team winning two of three games.
- **Timed games.** In large 3 v 3 tournaments or round-robin competition, time is limited to keep the competition running smoothly. Depending on the number of teams and courts available, 8- to 10-minute games are typical times. Timed games may use side-out or rally scoring. In both side-out and rally scoring, teams change sides at eight points in the deciding game. Note that in table 7.1 on page 67 we recommend rally scoring for all games and all age groups. This method of scoring is exciting for the kids and is swift, helping to keep games and matches on schedule. However, be sure to inform your players about side-out scoring.

Game Play

Here we will look at rules that govern game play, including serving, contacting the ball during play, net play, and faults.

Serving

The first serve of game 1 is decided by a coin toss; games 2 and 3 will be started with a serve by the team that did not serve first in the previous game. Players must follow the service order. When the serving team wins the rally, the player who served on that point serves again. When the receiving team wins the rally, it gains the right to serve and rotates clockwise.

The server may move freely in the service zone, which runs the entire width of the court (and must be completely in the service zone and not touching the court (including the endline) or the playing surface outside the zone at the moment of contact or takeoff for a jump serve. When the official blows a whistle for the serve, a player has eight seconds to serve the ball.

A player is allowed one service tossing error (letting the ball bounce without hitting it after tossing it up for a serve) per serve. Serve faults happen when the ball

- touches a player of the serving team,
- fails to pass over the net,
- lands out of bounds, or
- passes over a screen.

A screen occurs when one or more players waves arms, jumps, or moves sideways, hiding the server as the ball is being served.

We recommend that, before players are formally taught to underhand serve, they be allowed to use either a free-ball toss serve or an underhand serve. If they serve underhand and a serve fault occurs, they are allowed a second serve and may opt to use a free-ball toss for that serve.

Contacting the Ball During Play

The following rules govern contacting the ball during play:

- Each team may have three successive contacts to return the ball to the opponent's area. If the first touch is on a block, the team may have three additional contacts to return the ball.
- The ball may contact any part of the body and any number of body parts as long as it does so simultaneously.
- When the ball comes to rest momentarily in the hands or arms of a player, it is considered *held*. This is a violation.
- *Double contact* occurs when a player hits the ball more than once with no other player touching it between these contacts. However, a player who blocks the ball may touch it a second time without an intervening touch by another player.

- If the ball is held simultaneously by two opposing players, it is a *double fault* and results in a playover.
- If two players on the same team contact the ball simultaneously, this is considered as being two contacts for their team.
- A player who places any part of the body above the height of the net is considered to have the intention to block; only front-line players may block.
- If two players contact the ball on a block, it is considered only one hit.
- Blockers may reach over the net to block the ball as long as the opponents have hit the ball in such a manner that the ball would clearly cross the net if not touched by a defending player.
- Only front-line players are allowed to spike or return the ball with their hands in a position higher than the top of the net from in front of the attack line (see figure 7.1 on page 67).
- Back-line players may not block and may spike only when they take off (jump) from behind the attack line.

Net Play

Several rules govern play near the net and at the centerline:

- The ball must pass from one side of the net to the other over the legal portion of the net.
- The ball remains in play if it touches the legal portion of the net in play. (*Note:* A rule instituted in 2000 allows the ball to remain in play if it touches the top of the net during the serve.)
- A player may not touch the net during play except for insignificant contact by a player not in the act of playing the ball.
- If the ball is driven into the net with such force that it contacts an opponent, this is not a net fault.
- The hands may legally pass over the net after a spike on the follow-through.
- The only parts of the body allowed to touch the opponent's court are the feet; however, some part of the foot or feet must remain on or above the centerline at the time of contact.
- Players can cross the *vertical plane* (an imaginary continuation of the net above and below its actual limits) as long as they don't interfere with an opponent.

- A player may not spike the ball until part of the ball is on that player's side of the net.

Officials

Volleyball officials usually are volunteers, not professionals. As a volunteer yourself, you surely understand and appreciate the difficult but important role officials play in youth sport. We hope you will remember this volunteer spirit as you react to an official's decisions during a match. How you react when you think an official has made a mistake is very important. Be a good role model for your players and their parents. If you think a rule was not properly enforced, raise the issue calmly or ask your floor captain to speak to the official for a clarification. It is *never* appropriate to scream or berate an official's character.

Remember, volleyball is for players to learn skills in a fun and motivating atmosphere. Do what you can to create this type of atmosphere as you coach and as you work with officials. Your players and their parents will learn a lot about being good sports by emulating your coaching behavior. Figure 7.7 shows the various official calls.

Officials enforce the rules of the game, and they make sure players participate within the spirit of the rules. Players or coaches who commit any of the following actions will cause their team to be given an individual or team penalty:

- Making rude or vulgar remarks or gestures
- Engaging in disruptive or distracting behavior during the game from outside the court
- Yelling, shouting, or clapping at an opponent who is playing or attempting to play a ball

Figure 7.7 Officiating signal for: *(a)* side out, *(b)* ball in bounds/line violation, *(c)* ball out, *(d)* ball contacted by player and going out of bounds, *(e)* four hits, *(f)* crossing the centerline, *(g)* held, thrown, lifted, or carried ball, *(h)* double hit, *(i)* beckoning the serve, *(j)* substitution, *(k)* ball served into the net or player touching the net, *(l)* over the net, *(m)* double fault or play over, *(n)* illegal block or screen, *(o)* point.

Figure 7.7 *(continued)*

chapter 8

Tactics and Skills

As your athletes play games in practice, their experiences in these games—and your subsequent discussions with them about their experiences—will lead them to the tactics and skills that they need to develop to succeed. In the games approach to teaching, tactics and skills go hand in hand.

In this chapter, we'll provide information for you to teach your players offensive and defensive team tactics and individual skills. We'll also include suggestions for identifying and correcting common errors. Remember to use the IDEA approach to teaching skills—Introduce, Demonstrate, and Explain the skill, and Attend to players as they practice the skill. For a refresher on IDEA, see chapter 5. If you aren't familiar with volleyball skills, rent or purchase a video to see the skills performed. You may also find advanced books on skills helpful.

We've only provided information about the basics of volleyball in this book. As your players advance in their volleyball skills, you'll need to advance in your knowledge as a coach. You can do so by learning from your experiences, watching and talking with more experienced coaches, and studying advanced resources.

Offensive Tactics

An accurate pass to the setter, a well-executed set, and a hard-driven attack are keys to success in volleyball. The offense begins with a set to a hitter and an attack over the net. Teams that can control the ball through setting and hitting will reduce the number of errors and have better chances to score points and maintain the serve.

But the offense can't start until the team plays solid defense and passes an opponent's serve or digs an opponent's spike. And serve reception and digging—two skills of defensive transition—are essential to enabling the offense to develop. Later in this chapter, we will cover defense and defensive transition skills. But before that discussion, we will describe a team's offense once the ball has been passed or dug up after the opponent's serve or attack.

Offensive Alignments

After your team has successfully received a serve or volley from the opponent, it assumes the offense. When your team takes the offense, its members will be working to set up a well-placed or hard-driven spike back over the net. In the following sections, you'll see how to align your team's offense to fit the type of defense it faces.

If the opponents are blocking your attack, your players should cover any possible tips or deflections. If no block is present, your offensive alignment will change to prepare for the defensive transition. The next sections describe the player alignments (which work on any playing surface) for either situation: with or without a block.

Three-Player Offensive Alignments

We suggest that 8- and 9-year-olds play in a three-on-three league, 10- and 11-year-olds play in four-on-four, and older players play six-on-six. Even if your team plays in a six-on-six league, practicing three-on-three will give your players more opportunities for ball contact and, therefore, skill learning. We will first discuss how to align your players

Error Detection and Correction for Team Offense

ERROR Players stand around without communicating to one another when a ball comes between them. Attacks or serves hit the floor, and the players blame one another for not playing the ball.

CORRECTION Players should always be in a flexed ready position, prepared to go after a ball hit in their direction. Those who can play the ball while moving in the direction of the target have priority in playing it. Others should turn to watch their teammates hit the ball and should be ready to play an errant pass. Players should practice calling "Mine!" anytime the ball is hit to them.

for the offense in simpler situations of three-on-three and then give the adjustments for the more traditional six-on-six games.

Offensive Alignment Without a Blocker. Your team can take advantage of an opposing team that does not put a blocker up at the net, thus defending against the opponent's immediate return. As figure 8.1 shows, the passer (P) first passes to the setter (S). The hitter (H) is in the hitting position, awaiting the setter's set. As the hitter attempts to attack the set from the setter, the setter may step off the net and prepare for the opponent's return. After passing to the setter, the passer looks to see if

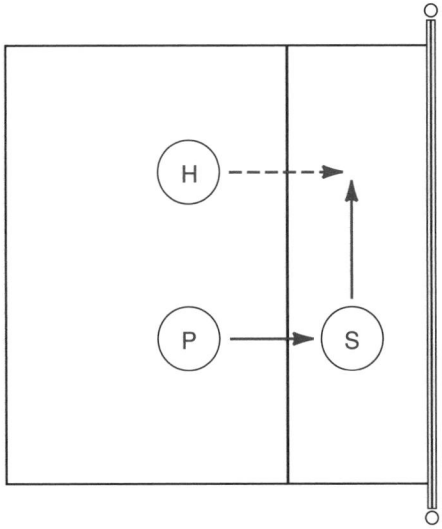

Figure 8.1 Three-on-three offensive alignment without a blocker.

the hitter has a blocker and then prepares to assist in the event of the opponent's return when the hitter hits the offensive attack. If the hitter passes the first ball, the setter will still set, and the passer can assume the hitting role on the third (next) contact.

Offensive Alignment With a Blocker. With a blocker in place against your offensive alignment, you should make minor adjustments to provide coverage against a block that may deflect back into your court. If your hitter (H) faces a blocker (B) when going for the hit, the passer (P) and the setter (S) should move in closer to the hitter to cover the ball that the opponent blocks (see figure 8.2).

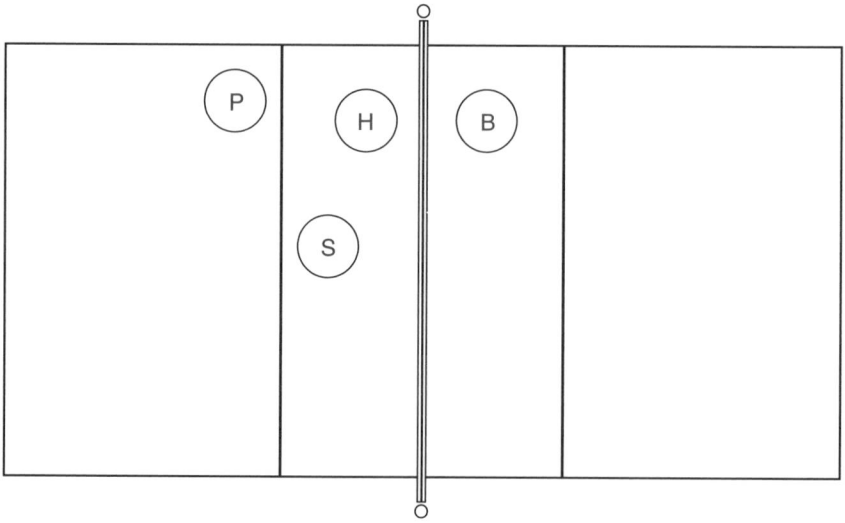

Figure 8.2 Three-on-three offensive alignment with a blocker.

Players must learn to see if the other team has a blocker at the net. In coaching, emphasize the importance of team members' communicating with one another as they move into position and set the ball up for the hitter at the net. The teammates who are covering the hitter should be in a low and balanced position ready to pursue the ball in any direction. Although making the adjustment for a blocker at the net is not difficult, it is essential to an effective offense.

Six-Player Offensive Alignments

Offensive alignments in six-on-six volleyball are more complex because more players are on the court. Every one of these players must understand her personal responsibilities on the court as well as what responsibilities teammates hold. Figure 8.3a and b illustrates coverage positions for all six players. Emphasize to your players that although these alignments are not always possible, they are desirable. If players cannot get to these positions (as shown in figure 8.3a and b), they should stop as soon as the attacker makes the contact and anticipate that a ball will deflect off the opponent's block. The players closest to the attacker probably will have the most opportunities to respond to a blocked ball, but

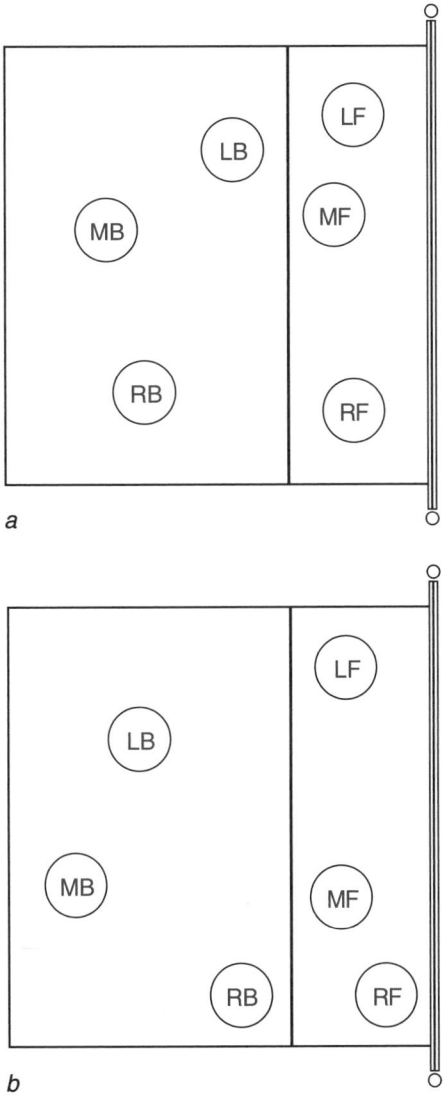

Figure 8.3 Six-on-six offensive alignment: *(a)* left-side attack and *(b)* right-side attack.

the players who are farther away must also be ready for and alert to balls deflected deep into the court.

Offensive Alignment Without a Blocker. If the opponent chooses not to block, the alignment for a six-player offense will be similar to the three-person format. Assuming the opponents dig the attack, the players with defensive responsibility can "cheat" their way back to their defensive positions with little threat of their teammate's attack getting blocked. In the six-player game, the setter will be played by the middle-front player, eliminating confusion as to who should set the attacker and allowing the other players to focus on their areas of responsibility.

Offensive Alignment With a Blocker. Whether your opponents use one or two blockers, you'll need to adjust your strategy. The likelihood of your team's attack getting blocked has increased, and all players should share the responsibility of covering the ball when the block occurs. Most balls are blocked in front of the 10-foot line, so your alignment should protect that immediate area around the attacker. If the left-front attacker receives the set, the setter and left back will share equal responsibility in picking up the ball blocked 10 feet or closer to the net. If the right-front player receives the set, then the setter and right-back player will have primary responsibility.

It is critical that all other players assume positions to protect the majority of the court, defending against balls that land elsewhere. A basic rule in covering the court is that a backcourt defender should never be directly behind or beside a teammate. If the players follow this rule, the court will be balanced in defensive coverage.

Set-Hit Combinations

The ultimate goal of a volleyball team on offense is to complete the three-hit sequence of pass, set, and attack. Your team must convert a hard-driven serve into a ball that is easily managed. This requires your players to cushion the ball as they receive it and to direct it high and "easy" to the setter.

Three basic sets to set up an attack are the high-outside set, the quick set, and the back set. The high-outside set is placed on the left side of the court so that, if left alone, it would drop on the left sideline. It is set at least six feet higher than the top of the net. In the high-outside set, it is the attacker's responsibility to go to the ball. The attacker should wait for the set to be half the distance to him or her from the setter before moving toward the set. The attacker should then approach the net, covering the distance with as few steps as possible. The last two steps are most important in preparing to make a two-footed jump before hitting the ball.

The quick set is always set in relation to the setter. The setter sets the ball directly in front of herself and one to two feet higher than the top of the net. In a quick set, it is the setter's responsibility to set the ball accurately to the attacker. The attacker approaches in front of the setter and jumps before or as the setter contacts the ball.

The back set needs less traveling distance than the high-outside set and requires less height (five to six feet higher than the top of the net). The back set is performed with the same technique as the overhead pass except that as the setter contacts the ball, she arches her back and directs the ball toward the ceiling. A good setter prepares to execute all sets exactly the same way to avoid giving the opponent any indication of the intended set (see figure 8.4).

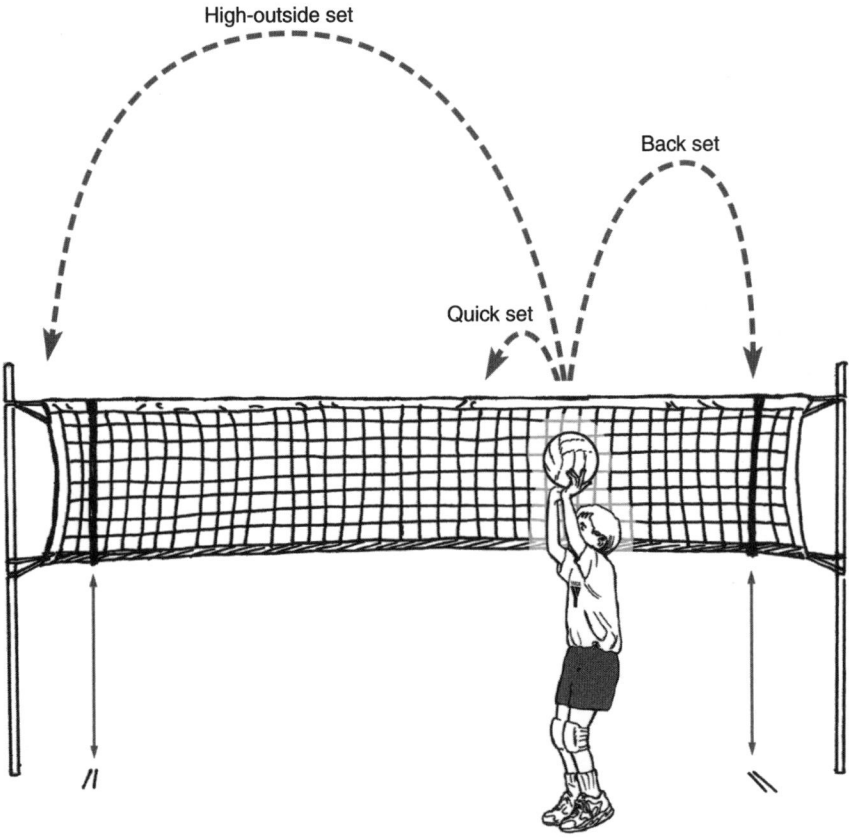

Figure 8.4 Ball paths for the high-outside, quick, and back sets. The tape markers on the net are located directly over the sidelines.

Set-Hit Combination Game

THREE HITS

Goal

To use a three-hit attack (forearm passing, overhead passing, hitting) to hit the ball over the net.

Description

The game is played 4 v 4 (see figure 8.5). Team A serves to team B. Award three points if the ball goes over the net after the three-hit pattern (forearm, overhead, hit) is performed. Play is continuous. Award one point to the team that wins the rally. Alternate serves between the two teams, regardless of who wins the rally. Rotate players after each rally.

To make the game easier:

- Have the coach hit easy serves or have the players toss the ball.
- Award points for any three hits that result in the ball's clearing the net.
- Award one point for a three-hit attack, even if the third hit does not clear the net or goes out of bounds.
- Play 5 v 5.

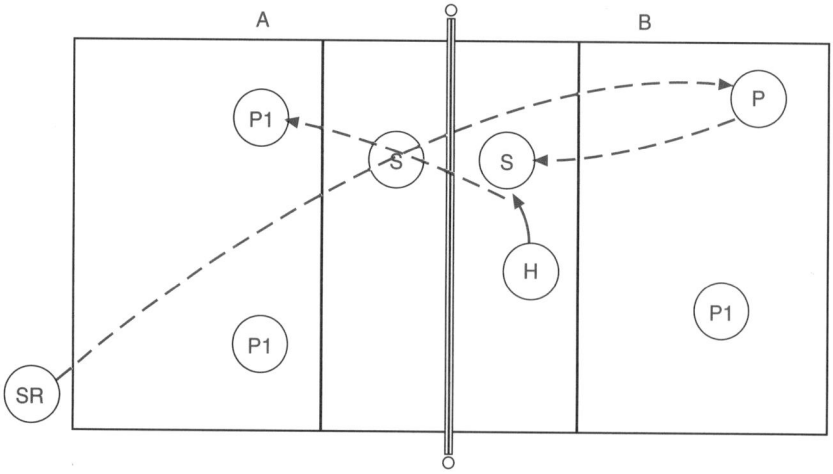

Figure 8.5 Three Hits.

To make the game harder:

- Only award the three points if the ball stays in the court after the three hits.
- Play 3 v 3.

Defensive Tactics

Every time your team passes a serve or digs an attack, it is playing defense. Without good team defense (which includes digging and blocking coverage), your team will not be able to execute an effective offense. Once your players know the forearm pass, teaching them team defense is mostly a matter of positioning. You want to put your players in the best position to counter whatever your opponent's offense is doing.

Being aware of youngsters' playing tendencies helps when you teach team defense. Most young attackers prefer to hit crosscourt rather than down the line. Figure 8.6 shows what cross-court and down-the-line mean. For example, an opponent's left-side attacker will hit cross-court, meaning in most cases that the left-back player will be the most likely digger of the attack. If the opponent's right-side spiker is the attacker, the right-back player will probably become the digger. To prepare your defensive positioning, therefore, you would align your diggers so that

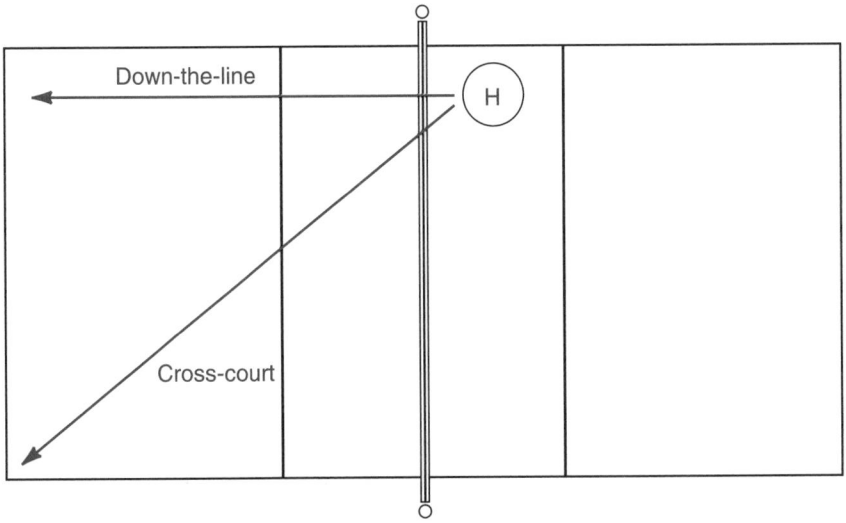

Figure 8.6 Hitting cross-court versus hitting down-the-line.

they are prepared for the cross-court attack. Young athletes will be confused as to what position they are in (cross-court or down-the-line), and you'll want to spend ample time defining the positions and reminding them about these defensive concepts for positioning.

Serve-Receive Considerations

The most common serve-receive alignments are the two-player serve-receive and the three-player serve-receive. Whichever alignment you use, many of the serves in youth volleyball tend to drop between the passers. A good rule to determine who should pass the ball is this: The passer who can move toward the target and pass should be the player who passes. A player who tries to receive a serve while moving away from the target will have difficulty controlling the pass and directing it to the target. In figure 8.7, for example, the passer (P) should pass the serve instead of the hitter (H). The hitter would be moving away from the setter (S), who is the target, to play the ball, whereas the passer will be moving forward and toward the setter.

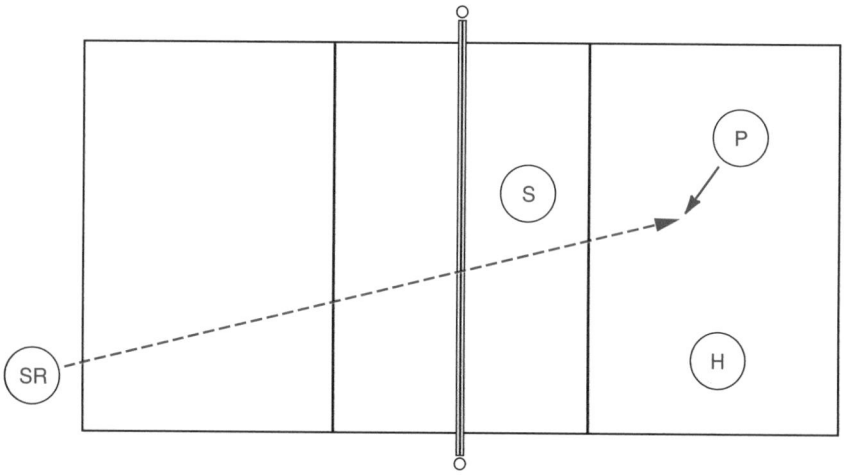

Figure 8.7 The player moving toward the target is the one who should pass the ball.

Two-Player Serve-Receive

If your opponent has a weak serving game (that is, few serves that are hard hits or difficult to pass), you can use the two-player serve-receive. Many people think that passing with only two people is not enough, especially with young players. The two-player serve-receive gives those two people responsibility for every serve that crosses the net. Passing with more than two players often leads to breakdowns in communication as more people try to simultaneously communicate their decisions.

In three-on-three volleyball, two players are positioned back in the court to receive the serve (passer [P] and passer/hitter [P/H]), while the third, the setter (S), is at the net preparing to set the pass (see figure 8.8). The object for the passer and the passer/hitter is to pass the serve to the setter without causing the setter to move very far. The better the passer and the passer/hitter become at passing, the easier it will be for the setter to set a good ball for the third contact. The setter is not involved in receiving the serve in this two-player alignment. As long as the passer and the passer/hitter can handle the opposition's serves, the setter is in a very favorable court position to set and initiate the offensive attack.

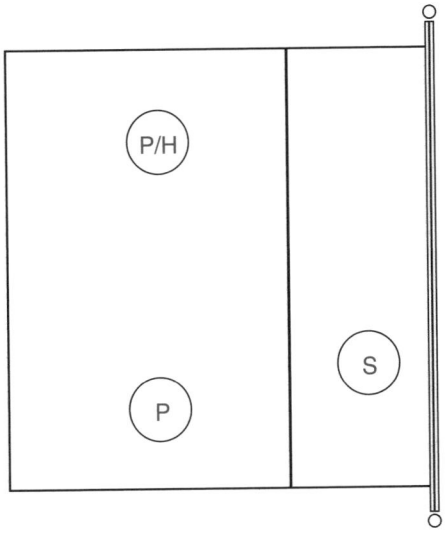

Figure 8.8 Three-on-three two-player serve-receive.

Figure 8.9 (page 92) illustrates the placement of a two-person serve-receive in six-on-six volleyball. In most cases the left-back (LB) and right-back (RB) players will be the two youngsters receiving serves, and they will be passing to the setter (MF). Notice that the serve could still be played by the middle-back player (MB), but the emphasis will be on the left- and right-back players (LB and RB) passing the serves.

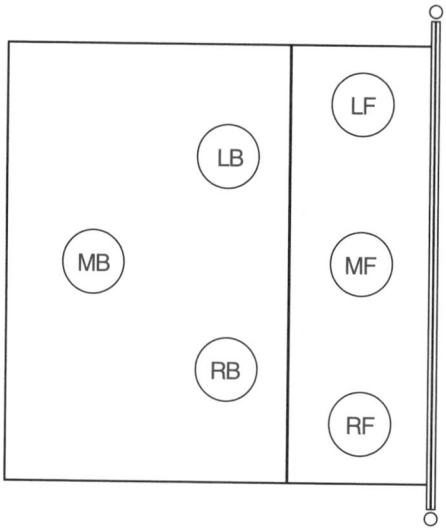

Figure 8.9 Six-on-six two-player serve-receive.

Three-Player Serve-Receive and Five-Player Serve-Receive

If your team is having difficulty receiving the serve (the ball goes erratically out of bounds or doesn't reach the setter), you can move players into a three-player serve-receive (for 4 v 4) or a five-player serve-receive (for 6 v 6). These alignments put the maximum number of players in position to receive the serve, leaving only the setter as a nonreceiver. With more passers involved, however, communication becomes even more important. Lack of communication can quickly erase the advantages the three- and five-player serve-receives should provide. In most situations, the serve-receivers will have comparable passing ability. Sometimes, however, one passer will be slightly better. In such an instance, give this passer more responsibility, having the player pass on a greater area of the court. Just make sure that the other passers are aware of this!

Communication continues to be vital. Passers should always call, "Ball!" or, "Mine!"—even when it might seem obvious to the player pursuing the ball. Balls that are served between two passers require even more communication. The basic rule to follow when the ball is served between two passers is this: The passer who can move into the seam (the space between two players) and move in the direction of the target should take the ball. If your team members learn to recognize this kind of situation and communicate their intentions, they will succeed in three- and five-player serve-receives.

To help decide whether to use a two-, three-, or five-person serve-receive, consider these circumstances. First, if you have three comparable passers, use them. To pass effectively with only two team members, you need skilled passers with above-average abilities to move and anticipate action. Second, if you are coaching beginners, opt for more serve-receivers; they will get more opportunities to practice the skill of serve reception. Last, if the movement skills your players have still are not developed, choose the three- or five-person serve-receive—it will be more effective.

In three-on-three volleyball, three players can cover the court and defend the short serve (see figure 8.10a, page 94) or long serve (see figure 8.10b) more effectively. Figure 8.10a shows all three players close to the net, anticipating a short serve. The setter (S) is in position to receive a short serve in the middle, the hitter (H) at the short line, and the passer (P) at the short crosscourt angle. In figure 8.10b, the setter moves to cover the crosscourt long serve. The hitter and the passer cover the long line and the long middle-serving angles. Since the setter is the least likely to receive the long serve (this angle is the most difficult for a server to hit), she is in the best possible position to set the second ball from the hitter or the passer. If the setter receives the first contact, the passer or the hitter becomes the setter.

In six-on-six volleyball, the three-player serve-receive is similar to the two-player serve-receive. Figure 8.11 shows that the middle-back passer (MB) is the third person to be incorporated into the serve-receive. In serve receptions, instruct the middle-back passer to take responsibility for the deep serves. In a five-player serve-receive, all but the setter should be prepared to receive the serve (see figure 8.12). Teams who pass the serve consistently keep their opponents from scoring on the serve; they also generate their own offensive attack from their good team defense.

Defensive Alignments

Some teams depend on their hitters to make aggressive attacks that score points. Others prefer to mix up their attacks by hitting hard-driven spikes combined with off-speed hits or tips. As you coach, you should watch for times when it might be wise to adjust your team's defensive alignments to fit the type of attacks the opponent is hitting. Defensively, you must decide your team's strategy based on how your players can best counter the opponent's strengths. As you now know, most attackers hit crosscourt. Unless you see opponents who can consistently hit more areas, assume that crosscourt hitting will frequently occur.

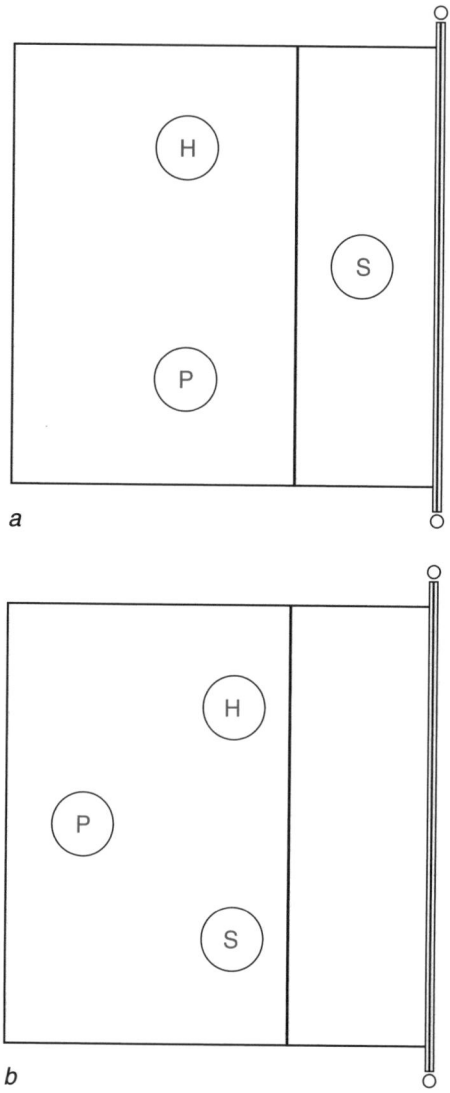

Figure 8.10 Three-on-three three-player serve-receive of *(a)* a short serve and *(b)* a long serve.

In developing your strategies, you face two basic decisions. You must decide whether to block and whether to use a free-ball alignment. Here are a few guidelines to help you decide. Before you choose to use a block, make sure you have blockers who can get their wrists over the net. Players who can't extend over the net will not be effective blockers.

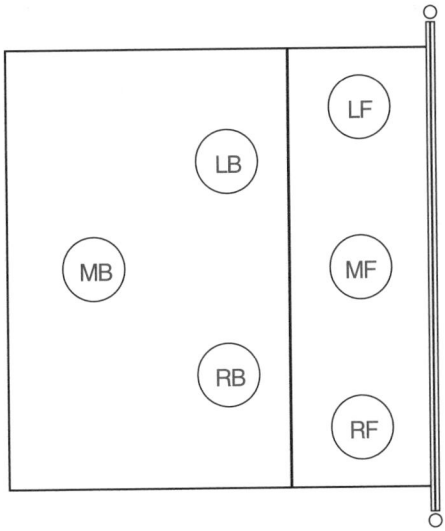

Figure 8.11 Six-on-six three-player serve-receive.

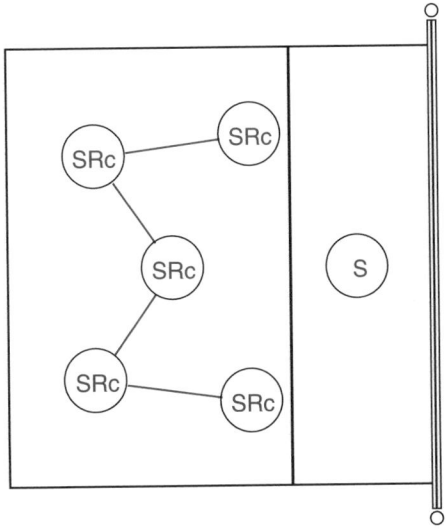

Figure 8.12 Serve-receive.

When you choose to incorporate a block, in effect you have decided that the opponents are capable of putting the ball down effectively. Opponents whose teams have bigger athletes or youngsters who are especially skilled as passers and hitters probably can put the ball down effectively. Moreover, choosing to block means you think you have players with the blocking ability to make significant contributions to your team's success.

Playing a defense without a block is often the better decision. If your players cannot get their wrists over the net consistently, blocking will not be effective. And opponents who do not have skilled hitters probably do not warrant a blocking defense anyway. Furthermore, if your team is especially skilled at digging, you can accentuate that ability by choosing not to block. In the end, deciding whether to block depends largely on the players you are working with; determine what will be best for your team's players.

A free-ball alignment is best used when the opponent has little or no chance of putting the ball down on your defense. Free balls come over the net when the set is misdirected to the attacker or not even attacked by the offensive team, and they usually come over high and soft. A player on your opponent's team who is returning the ball with a forearm pass or set will not have a great likelihood of having the ball go to the floor on your side. The ball being returned is moving slowly and perhaps high, which gives your players ample time to move into position to play the ball. We will explain this alignment later in more detail.

Defense With a Block

Use a blocker to defend teams with a strong hitting attack. Adding blocking to your team defense will challenge opponents to either hit over or hit around the block. When blocking, either one or two players are at the net, and the other players are defending open spaces around the blocker.

Power-Spike Alignment. When your team is playing three-on-three volleyball against a team with an aggressive (power spike) hitting attack, your blocking alignment should focus primarily on stopping the power spike from crossing the net. As illustrated in figure 8.13, the setter (S) is at the net blocking, the hitter (H) covers the short angle that is open around the block, and the passer (P) covers any ball hit down the line. Balls hit over the block (the setter) will have a high trajectory, allowing time for the passer and the hitter to communicate and cover this area.

When your team is playing six-on-six volleyball against a team with a power-spike attack, align your players as in figure 8.14. In this alignment for a power spike coming from the opponent's left side, the middle-front (MF) and right-front (RF) players will block. The left-front (LF) player should be near the 10-foot line, covering any short balls off the block. Position the middle-back (MB) player, who will be responsible for balls hit deep or off the block, on the baseline. The left-back (LB)

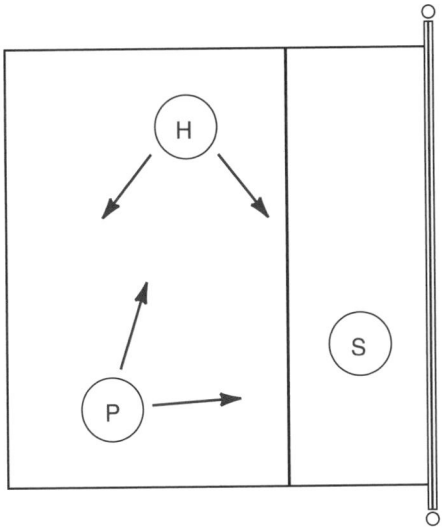

Figure 8.13 Three-on-three defensive alignment with a block against a power spike.

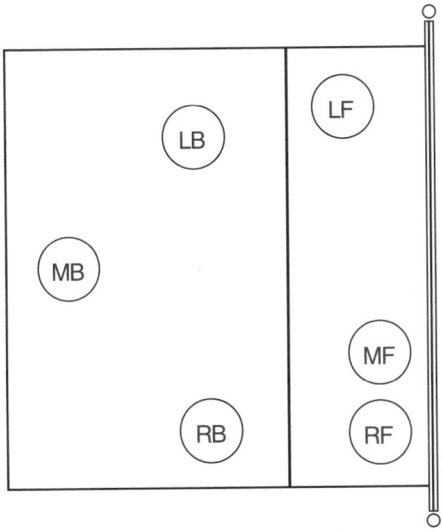

Figure 8.14 Six-on-six defensive alignment with a block against a power spike.

and right-back (RB) players should be about 18 feet from the net and close to their respective sidelines; their movements will be primarily forward.

Off-Speed Hit Alignment. Opponents who "read" (see) your block may use an off-speed hit to avoid it. An off-speed hit will not have maximal force, as it's a soft hit placed to a part of the court with no defenders. The defensive alignment to use against the off-speed hit puts your players in position to dig this attack effectively. In three-on-three volleyball, you would position the setter (S) at the net to attempt to block or deflect any type of offensive attack. The passer (P) moves in to cover the off-speed hit or tip just behind the setter's block. The hitter (H) covers the backcourt area for any long off-speed hits or tips (see figure 8.15).

Communication is essential in this type of defense. Who will play the ball depends largely on where it is placed and who has the best angle to make the play. Watching the attacker is usually the best way for the defense to know what to do.

Players who have slow approaches or who have been blocked consistently will look to tip or off-speed hit in hopes of scoring points. While the off-speed attack can be used as an effective offensive weapon, it more typically is used when attackers lack confidence that they can attack the ball around the block.

In six-on-six volleyball, the off-speed hit alignment is essentially the same as the power-spike alignment. The only difference between them is the position of the left-front digger (LF). This player should assume more responsibility for digging the off-speed attack since these attacks

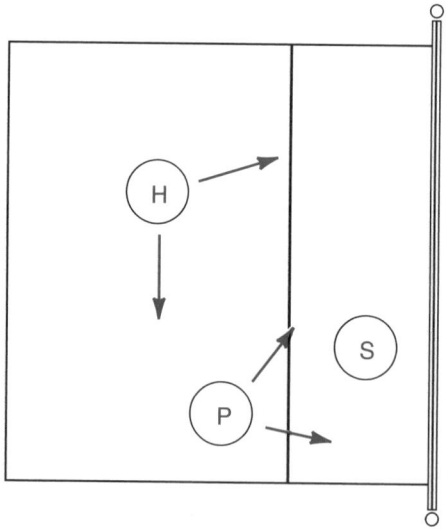

Figure 8.15 Three-on-three defensive alignment with a block against an off-speed hit.

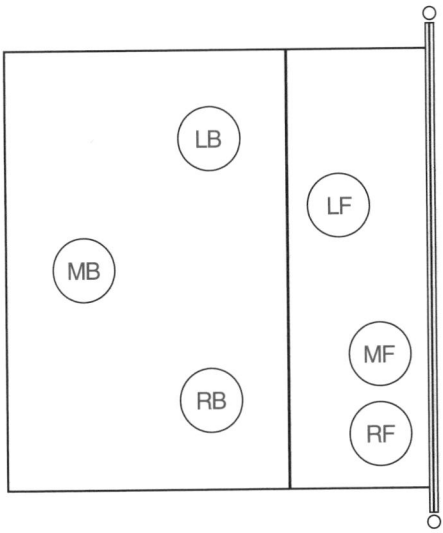

Figure 8.16 Six-on-six defensive alignment with a block against an off-speed hit.

primarily are directed to the middle of the court (see figure 8.16). Recognizing the off-speed attack is critical to defending against it! An opponent's attacker who approaches slowly or whose arm swings slowly is likely to hit an off-speed shot. Players who have consistently been blocked also are likely to try an off-speed attack to avoid getting blocked again. Encourage your players to pursue the off-speed attack on their feet and to try to stay off the ground.

Defense Without a Block

Suppose you have decided, either because your players can't get their wrists over the net or because your opponents are hitting a lot of free balls, that you do not need to use a block in your team defense. You have made a good decision, but now you must consider just where to position your players to defend against the attackers who do not have to hit around your block. Remembering that the attackers tend to hit crosscourt, even if there is no block up, will help you determine where to place your defenders.

There are three different alignments you will need to teach your players when they're playing without a block: free-ball alignment, power-spike alignment, and off-speed hit alignment. These alignments correspond to and prepare your players to defend against the three varieties of offensive attacks.

Free-Ball Alignment. Free balls are usually hit high, soft, and deep. A block will not be effective in defending a free-ball attack. In three-on-three volleyball with no block, all three players are free to help pass the ball. The hitter (H) moves back to cover the crosscourt angle (see figure 8.17). The passer (P) covers the middle of the court, and the setter (S) backs off the net, awaiting the pass from either the hitter or the passer to start the offensive attack. On a high, soft free ball, the hitter and the passer should have sufficient time to get to the ball and make the defensive dig.

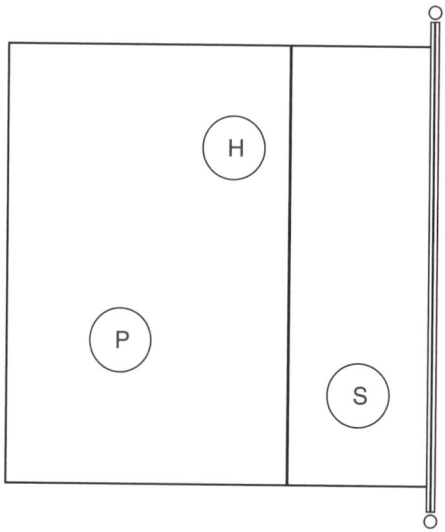

Figure 8.17 Three-on-three free-ball defensive alignment.

For six-on-six volleyball, you'll deploy your players in more of a spread arrangement for a free-ball alignment (see figure 8.18). Instruct your left-front (LF) and right-front (RF) players to pull off, or back from, the net to the 10-foot line to play any free ball that starts to land in front of them. Any ball going deeper into their court should be played by the backcourt players; they will balance the court with each responsible for one-third of the area.

Power-Spike Alignment. If your team is defending a power spike without a blocker in 3 v 3 volleyball, move your players back off the net in position to cover the angles of the court. The hitter (H) will cover the crosscourt angle; the setter (S), the attack down the line; and the passer (P), the area between these two angles (see figure 8.19). All three players should be in ready position to dig a hard-driven spike.

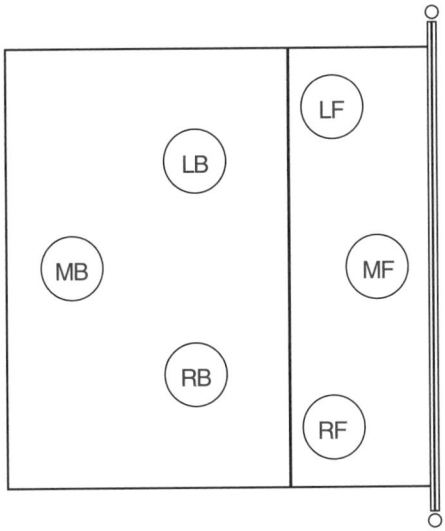

Figure 8.18 Six-on-six free-ball defensive alignment.

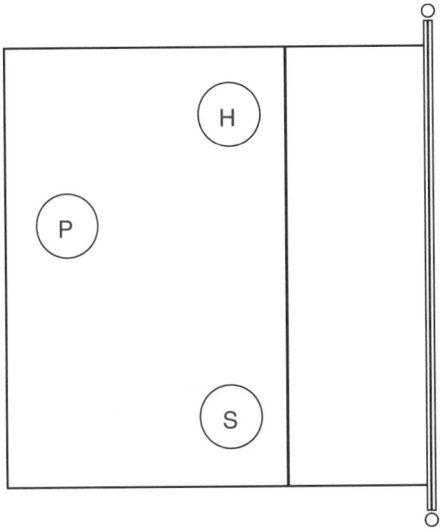

Figure 8.19 Three-on-three power-spike defensive alignment without a block.

With six players, the placement of the back row in a power-spike alignment is about the same without a blocker as with one (see figure 8.20). A primary difference between these blocking situations, however, is the flexibility your defenders should have. Without a block, the

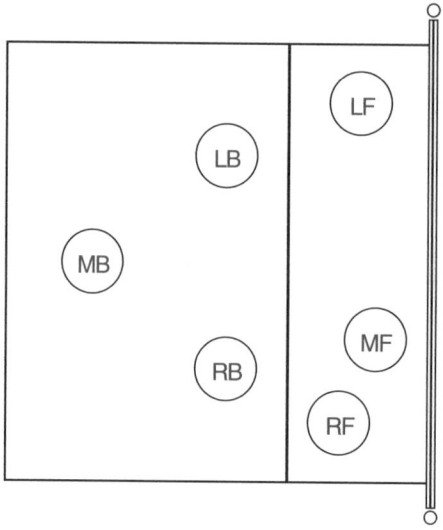

Figure 8.20 Six-on-six power-spike defensive alignment without a block.

back-row players need more freedom in making movements they think will effectively dig the opponent's attack. Be sure to set parameters for each back-row defender, however, so that no confusion arises among defenders as to who should dig a particular ball.

The placement of the front row also becomes important to consider, since these players will not be blocking. In figure 8.20, notice that the two front-row players closer to the point of attack (MF and RF) will pull off the net five to six feet to defend against off-speed attacks. The blocker farthest from the point of attack (LF) in essence becomes a back-row defender. Having the middle-front and right-front players responsible for off-speed attacks frees the back-row defenders to concentrate on any hard-driven spikes that go deep into their court.

Off-Speed Hit Alignment. To defend an off-speed hit or tip without a blocker at the net, players move in closer to the net to pick up short, soft hits. With three players, the hitter (H) covers the crosscourt angle, the setter (S) covers the short court (near the net), and the passer (P) plays the deep court (see figure 8.21). Opponents sometimes use the off-speed hit to throw the defensive team off balance. Remind your players to talk and call for the ball in making the first dig. In six-on-six volleyball, the off-speed and power-spike alignments are similar except that the left-front digger (LF) comes in three to four feet from the sideline (see figure 8.22). A good front row can see and dig the off-speed attack, and this is what you should hope to help your young players learn. Encour-

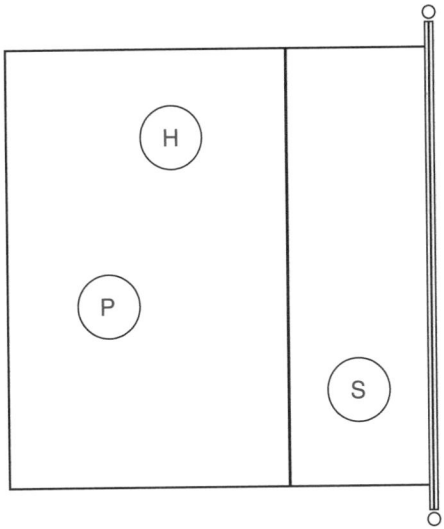

Figure 8.21 Three-on-three off-speed defensive alignment without a block.

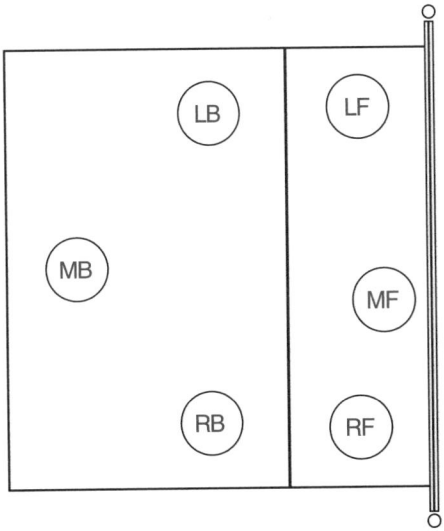

Figure 8.22 Six-on-six off-speed hit defensive alignment without a block.

age the back-row defenders to take responsibility for any off-speed attacks that fall between the front and back rows. A digger who is moving forward toward the ball has a better chance at making a well-placed dig.

Error Detection and Correction for Defensive Alignment

ERROR Players are frustrated in trying to dig a strong attack. The blocker is not effective in slowing down or altering the attack. Your nonblocking players are struggling to dig balls hit to them, and you can't seem to stop your opponent's offense.

CORRECTION Change to a three-player serve-receive and free-ball defensive alignment. This will put three players into position instead of two for the pass or dig. If your team has not thoroughly developed its blocking fundamentals, the three-person alignment gives players the best opportunity to cover the court defensively.

Base Position

The base defensive position is the position the team holds until a team leader determines whether the team should block or move into free-ball formation. In 3 v 3, players don't block; use a 0-3 alignment (see figure 8.23). In 4 v 4, use a 1-3 alignment with one player blocking (see figure 8.24). In 6 v 6, use either a 1-0-5 or a 1-1-4 alignment (see figures 8.25 and 8.26) before moving on to a 2-1-3 or a 2-4. Regarding blocking, teach players to observe opposing hitters to discern whether they need more than one blocker. Hitters that can't spike don't merit multiple blockers.

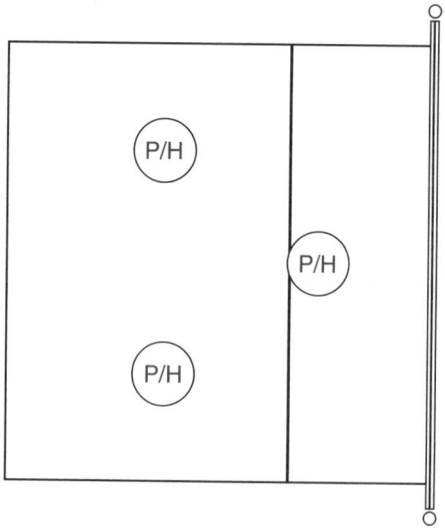

Figure 8.23 0-3 alignment.

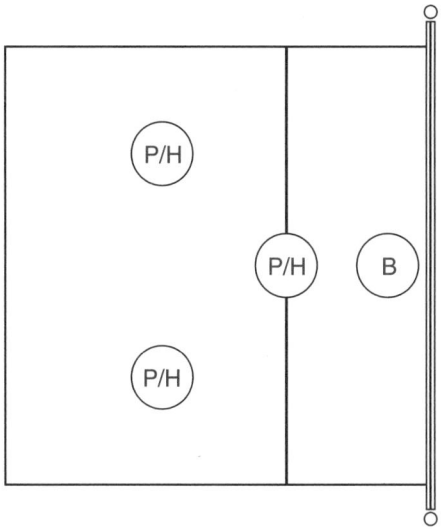

Figure 8.24 1-3 alignment.

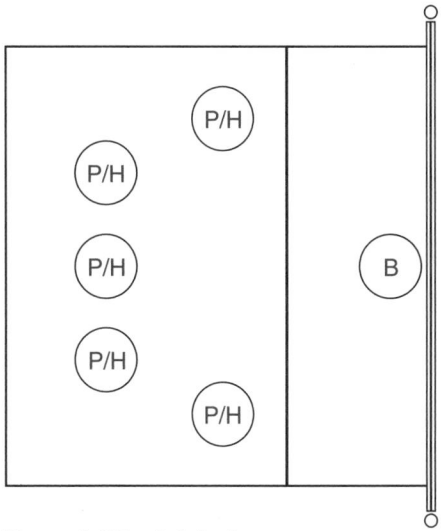

Figure 8.25 1-0-5 alignment.

The 2-1-3 is stronger against a team that uses tips and off-speed spikes, and the 2-4 is more effective against a powerful attacking team. In the 2-1-3 defense, the "2" represents the blockers, the "1" is a player who is positioned behind the block, and the "3" indicates the backcourt players. When you're using the 2-1-3 defense, the base position calls for the center-back player to be in the middle of the court. The two attackers

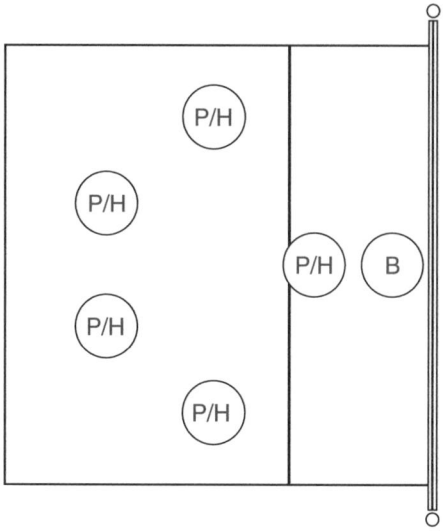

Figure 8.26 1-1-4 alignment.

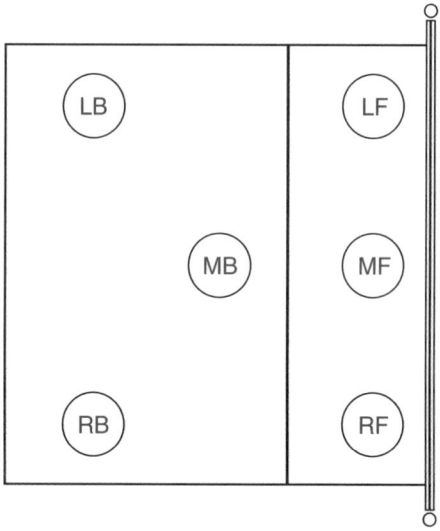

Figure 8.27 Base defensive formation for the 2-1-3 defense.

and the setter stay at the net, anticipating a block. The remaining two defensive players position themselves 15 to 20 feet from the net, close to their respective sidelines (see figure 8.27).

It is extremely important that all players on the team move into the same formation. Even if the team leader errs and calls, "Free ball," only to have the opposing team attack, the team is still capable of receiving the ball if everyone is in the same formation. If, however, some players block and others move to the free ball, some areas on the court will be very vulnerable. Figure 8.28 shows base defense to free-ball formation.

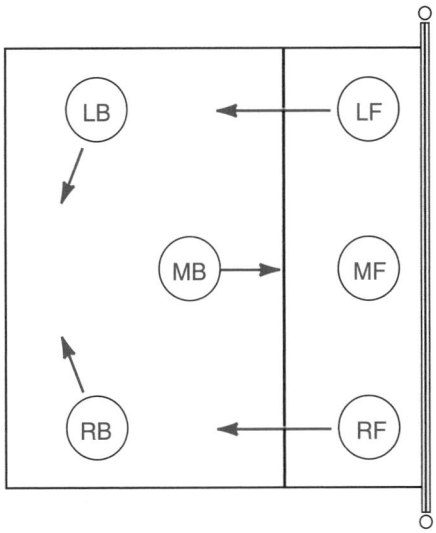

Figure 8.28 Movement to free-ball from base defensive formation.

Transitioning to Attack

In volleyball, the transition from defense to offense is swift—and the more efficiently the receiving team gets into its offense, the more likely they will set up an attack that will win a point. After learning the basic skills involved in attacking—forearm passing, setting or overhead passing, and hitting (also called spiking or attacking)—your team will be able to convert the opponent's attack or serve into its own attack. This conversion is referred to as transitioning to attack. The player receives the opponent's serve or hit, cushions it, and passes it high to the setter, who places the ball in position for the attack. While several types of sets may be used, high-outside sets will bring the most success for inexperienced players.

If your team is unable to make a swift and efficient transition to offense, it will be forced to return a free ball to its opponent. Teams that are continually forced to return free balls to opponents find themselves constantly on defense.

Error Detection and Correction for Transitioning to Attack

ERROR A ball dug by the setter does not get set.

CORRECTION The setter, after digging the attack, is not eligible to make the second contact or set; in this situation, the player in the right-front position assumes the setting role.

Opening Up

A common error in playing team defense is that players stand around without communicating to one another when a ball comes between them. Attacks or serves hit the floor, and the players blame one another for not playing the ball. As we have suggested earlier, players should practice calling, "Mine!" any time the ball is hit to them. Players can also communicate with teammates through body language by opening up (turning or pivoting as a ball is approaching) to signify to teammates that they are not playing the ball. Instead, they turn to watch a teammate hit the ball.

Individual Skills

Volleyball requires skills of mobility, balance, and jumping. This section will help you guide players in developing skills so that they can enjoy playing at any level. We'll emphasize these skills:

- Hitting
- Overhead passing
- Forearm passing
- Serving
- Serve-receiving
- Digging
- Blocking
- Pursuing and saving

Hitting

Pass, set, spike! Spiking a ball is one of the most thrilling plays at all levels. Once your players have the skills to set up a teammate for an attack, they will enjoy the excitement that great team play generates.

The attack is a general term used to describe how the ball is played over the net. The hit, or spike, is the primary skill used to attack the ball. A team that develops a strong attack will have opportunities to score points more readily.

Ready Position for Hitting

The ready position for an attack approach is slightly different from other ready positions. The spiker must turn and run back several steps from the net to have room for an approach to hit the ball explosively. The attacker should be standing in a relaxed position with arms comfortably at the sides. She should be at the side of the court, about 8 to 12 feet back off the net, waiting for the set (see figure 8.29).

Figure 8.29 Ready position for the attack (hit).

The Approach

The most common attack approach is a four-step pattern. Left-handed players start step one with the left foot; right-handers begin with the right foot (see figure 8.30a). A player needs an explosive movement from step two to step three to set up the quick foot plant into the jump (see figures 8.30b and c).

Figure 8.30 Proper technique for the attack approach.

The arms extend and swing straight back as high as possible on the third step. As the fourth (closure) step begins, the arms drive forward in a full sweeping motion to help drive the player off the ground to attack the ball (see figure 8.30d).

Body Position and Contact

In contacting the ball, think of the arm as a whip and the hand as the tip of that whip. The snap of the whip begins in the shoulder. The elbow of the hitting hand should be drawn back high and away from the shoulder (see figure 8.31a).

As contact is made, the hand should be firm and open, hitting the top half of the ball with the palm (see figure 8.31b).

Follow through quickly. In the follow-through, the arm should remain on the same side of the body (not crossing over the body), finishing

Figure 8.31 Proper technique for the attack contact.

behind the hitting-side leg. Remind your players that they will get a penalty for touching the net with any part of the body.

Various Types of Hits

The ball can be attacked in different ways. Each can be effective in scoring points. Usually, the harder the ball is hit, the less time opponents have to return the attack. However, teams can use other types of attacks with great success to keep opponents off balance. The following attacks are used in various game situations.

Hard-Driven Spike. This refers to a ball hit forcefully down into the opponent's court. The player contacts the ball with the heel of an open hand cutting into the center back. At contact, she forcibly snaps her wrist and drops her arm toward her waist. The wrist snap imparts topspin, causing the ball to drop quickly to the floor.

Off-Speed Spike. An off-speed spike is a controlled placement of the ball to an open space. It's performed with the palm of the hand with the same motion as a hard-driven spike, but instead of following through, the player slows or stops the arm and slows the wrist snap. The attacker may take a full swing but then let up and hit the ball softly to an open area.

Standing Spike. A standing spike, also called a down ball, is an attack used from a standing position to place the ball into the opponent's court. A player who doesn't have time for an approach or jump can hit a standing spike.

Open-Handed Tip. The open-handed tip is executed by gently directing the ball with the upper two joints of the fingers of the hitting hand, slightly in front of the hitting shoulder at full arm extension. The player contacts the ball slightly below the center back, directing the ball to barely clear the block and to drop quickly to the floor (see figure 8.32a-c).

Error Detection and Correction for Tipping

ERROR The ball goes into the net on a tip.

CORRECTION The player should contact the ball just in front of his hitting shoulder; the greater the distance the ball is in front of him, the lower it drops before contact and the greater the chance of its being hit into the net.

Figure 8.32 Proper technique for the open-handed tip.

Error Detection and Correction for Attacking

ERROR A player repeatedly hits the ball out of bounds or into the net. The player seems to lack body control.

CORRECTION The player must contact the ball at the peak of the jump. Check the approach and timing of the jump. Walk through the approach with your player. Remind him to watch the set to be able to judge when to approach for the hit. Have each player show you his arm swing from a standing position. Check that the elbow is away from the body and the palm of the hand is making good, solid contact on the ball. Emphasize speed over accuracy in the player's approach and arm swing. A player who both approaches and swings quickly will feel confident in learning the skill of attacking, even if the ball travels far out of the playing area.

Hitting Games

HAMMER TIME

Goal

To score points by spiking.

Description

The game is played 3 v 3 (see figure 8.33). Team A serves to team B, who uses a three-hit attack. Points are awarded when the ball is spiked. Award one point if the ball is spiked and hits the net or goes out; award two points if the ball is spiked and stays in play; and award three points if the ball is spiked and ends the rally. Play is continuous until the ball touches the ground. Alternate serves between teams, no matter who wins the rally, and give each team an equal number of serves. Rotate players after each rally.

Variation

This same game can be used to focus on other types of hits, such as crosscourt, down the line, or tip.

To make the game easier:

- Lower the net.
- Play 5 v 5 or 6 v 6.

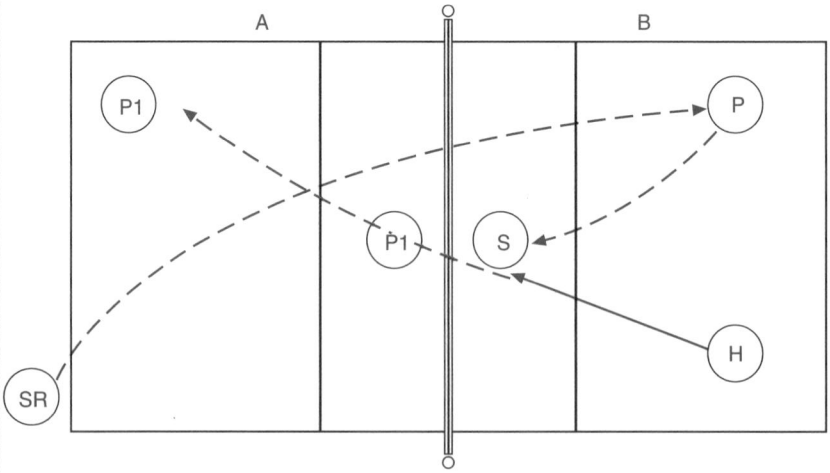

Figure 8.33 Hammer Time.

To make the game harder:

- Award points only for spikes that successfully end a rally.

SKEET SHOOTING

Goal

To increase hitting accuracy.

Description

The game is played 3 v 3. Divide the court into six zones with tape (see figure 8.34). The object is to hit the ball to one of those zones using a tip, hard-driven spike, off-speed spike, or down ball. The front zones and the center back zone are each worth one point; the back corner zones are each worth two points. Players begin the game with a set to a hitter. When a player hits a ball into a zone, award points. Allow players to use overhead passes or forearm passing to get the ball over the net, but award points only when balls are hit to the other side. Alternate setting to the hitter between teams, regardless of who wins the rally, and give each team an equal number of sets. Rotate players after each rally.

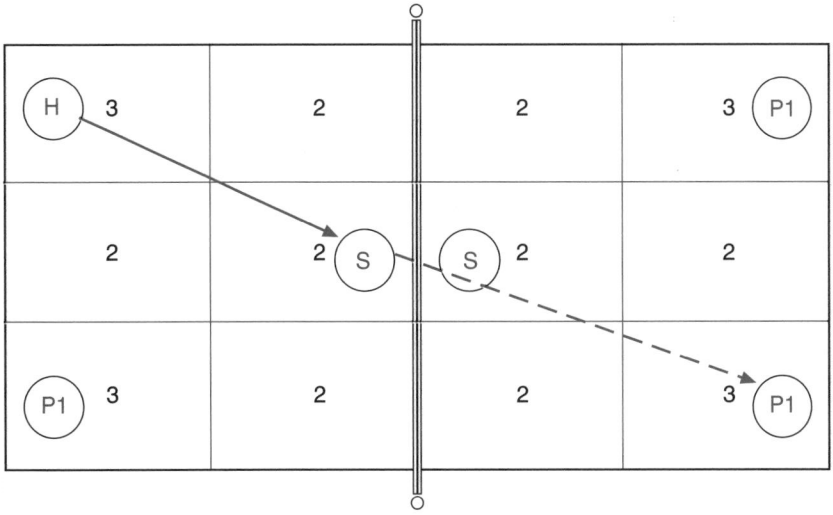

Figure 8.34 Skeet Shooting.

(continued)

Skeet Shooting *(continued)*

To make the game easier:

- Make the court larger.
- Lower the net.

To make the game harder:

- Have players call their hits and give them extra points if they accomplish this.
- Award points only if the ball hits the floor of the target zone.
- Use the nine-zone scoring system shown in figure 8.35.

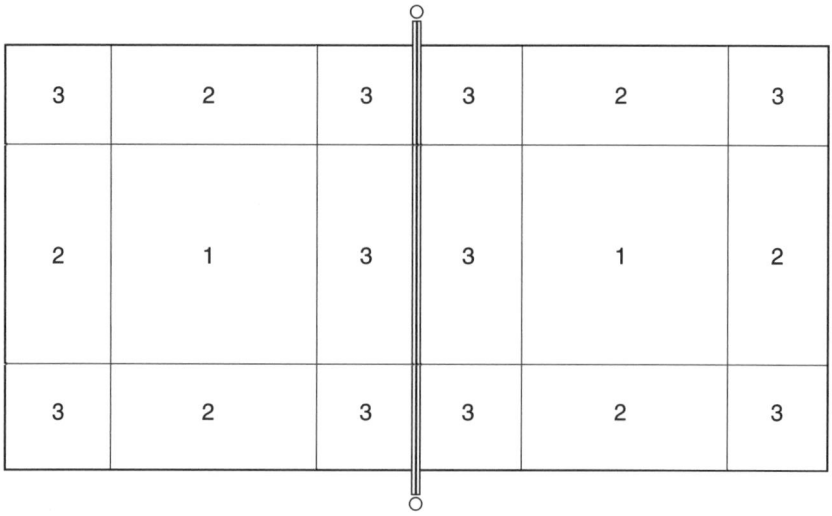

Figure 8.35 Nine-zone scoring system for Skeet Shooting.

Overhead Passing

The overhead pass may be used to play any ball that is moving high and slow, to set up an attack (usually referred to as a set), or to keep the ball in play when an attack is not possible. Instruct your players to use the overhead pass whenever appropriate, that is, when the ball is higher than shoulder level and coming to the player with little force. They shouldn't let the ball drop to forearm pass level, because the overhead pass is the most efficient way to handle the ball.

The best-known overhead pass is the set. The person directing the attack is called the setter, and the contact by the setter is called a set.

The setter, who can see the entire court from the net, determines which player is in the best position for an attack and places the ball where the attacker can aggressively hit the ball back to the opponent. Although the setter should be the best overhead passer on the team, all players at one time or another—whether they play the setter or another position—will use the overhead pass to play the ball.

Ready Position for Overhead Passing

Teaching players to make an overhead pass from the correct ready position is the first part of developing successful overhead passing. The player begins by standing facing the left side of the court with her feet shoulder-width apart, the right foot slightly ahead of the left. The knees should be bent slightly, and the weight should be on the balls of the feet. In this semicrouched position, the player will raise and cup her hands above the forehead, waiting for the ball (see figure 8.36).

Figure 8.36 Ready position for overhead passing.

Making the Pass

The player should shape her hands like the volleyball itself in front of the forehead and set to locate the ball through the "window" formed by the thumbs and forefingers. The wrists are cocked back and the fingers are spread and relaxed four to eight inches from the forehead as if holding a volleyball (see figure 8.37).

Figure 8.37 Proper hand position for overhead passing.

Players should contact the ball in the middle of the forehead (see figure 8.38a). The pads of the fingers, not the palm, should contact the ball (see figure 8.38b). Whenever possible, the player should square her shoulders to the target. As contact is made, the player should extend the arms and legs upward (see figure 8.38c).

The set is executed in the same manner as the overhead pass. The setter takes a position on the right side of the court, close to the net and facing the left sideline. The setter sets the ball to an attacker two to three feet off (away from) the net so that the attacker can hit the ball hard without contacting the net. Many beginning setters try to place the ball too close to the net, which does not allow the attacker the necessary angles to direct the attack around the opposing block. It is better to err on the side of setting too far away from the net rather than too close to it.

Figure 8.38 Proper technique for overhead passing.

Error Detection and Correction for Overhead Passing

ERROR The ball travels vertically instead of high and toward the target, or it does not reach the sideline.

CORRECTION Limb extension and weight transfer should be forward, toward the target. Contact the ball at its lower back, not its bottom. The player should make sure he extends his arms and legs faster for additional force if balls are not reaching the target.

Overhead Passing Games

SETTING PRETTY

Goal

To set up the attack through overhead passing.

Description

The game is played 3 v 3 (see figure 8.39). Award two points for overhead passes (sets) that can be reached by the hitters. Team A begins the game with an easy serve to team B. Play is continuous until the rally is won. Alternate serves between teams, regardless of who wins the rally, and give each team an equal number of serves. Rotate players after each rally.

To make the game easier:

- Play 4 v 4.

To make the game harder:

- Play 2 v 2.
- Award a point only if the set results in a winning hit.

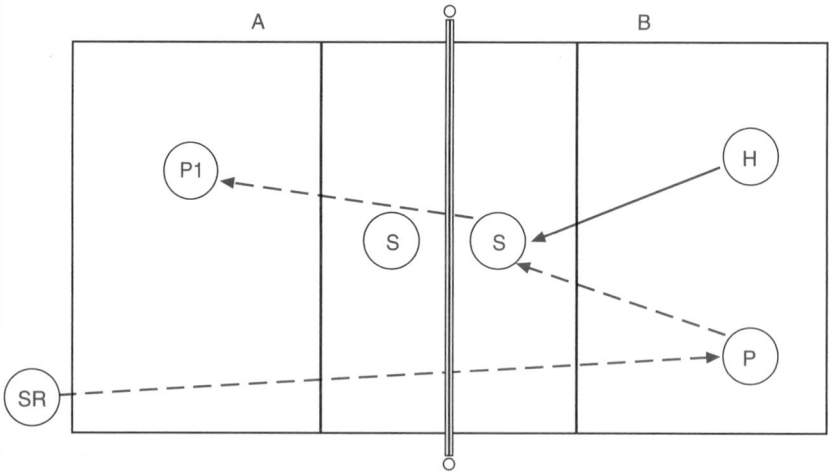

Figure 8.39 Setting Pretty.

PASS TO PARADISE

Goal

To set for a hit effectively using an overhead pass.

Description

The game is played 4 v 4 (see figure 8.40). Team A begins the game with an easy toss to team B. Give points only for hits made from overhead passes. Award one point for balls that go out, two points for balls that stay in but are hit back, and three points for balls that touch the floor or ground inbounds. Alternate tosses between teams, regardless of who wins the rally, and give each team an equal number of tosses. Rotate players after each rally.

To make the game easier:

- Play 5 v 5 or 6 v 6.

To make the game harder:

- Play 3 v 3.

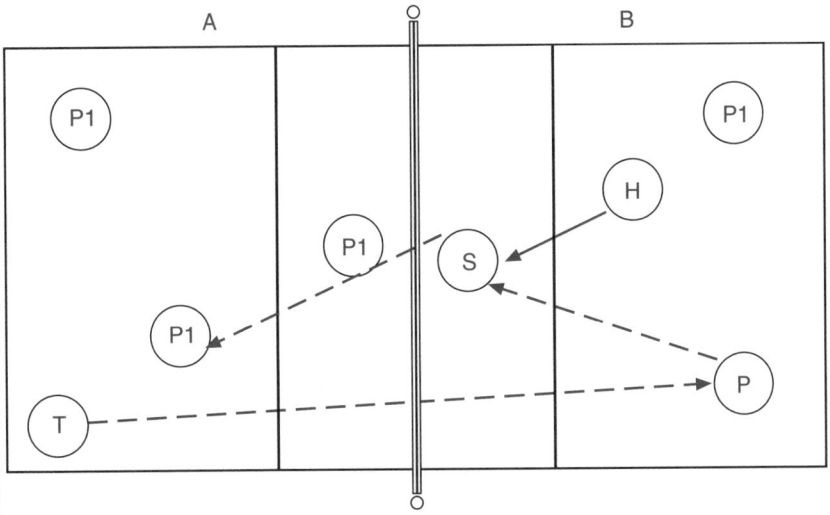

Figure 8.40 Pass to Paradise.

Forearm Passing

The forearm pass is for receiving hard-driven serves and spikes and for playing any ball that has gone into the net. Gaining control of the ball and accurately passing it to a teammate generates the offensive attack. If the ball is passed poorly, the setter will have difficulty placing the ball in the best position for the attacker.

Beginning players usually feel comfortable contacting the ball off their forearms. Some will complain of a "sting" as the ball hits their arms. But as their technique improves, they won't be hitting or swinging at the ball. Instead, they'll learn to soften and direct the passes.

Ready Position for Forearm Passing

All players must be able to pass a serve or dig a spike with the forearm pass. The forearm pass begins with a good ready position. From there, the player can execute the forearm pass and deliver the ball to the setter to begin the offense.

To learn the ready position for forearm passing, the player stand with her feet shoulder-width apart, toes turned in slightly, and the right foot just slightly ahead of the left. As she bends at the waist and flexes the knees, her weight should shift slightly forward onto the balls of the feet. Make sure that the head and shoulders are only slightly in front of the knees, and the arms are relaxed and extended in front of the body. Have the player keep the head up to follow the ball while keeping the knees bent and her weight over the balls of the feet (see figure 8.41).

Hand Position for the Forearm Pass

For the forearm pass, teach beginners to place their thumbs and palms facing close together. Figure 8.42 shows that when the thumbs and palms are together, an even platform is established. In all variations of the forearm pass, the hand position is important to ensure a flat surface with the forearms.

Platform Tilt

The platform tilt allows the player to direct his passes to a target (see figure 8.43). When unable to face the target squarely, the player can "dip" the shoulders and tilt the platform (the flat surface created by the forearms) to direct the ball accurately. The platform does not change (it remains flat), but the angle at which the ball hits and rebounds off the platform is adjusted to make the pass possible. After contact, the arms follow through, directing the ball to the target.

Figure 8.41 Ready position for forearm pass.

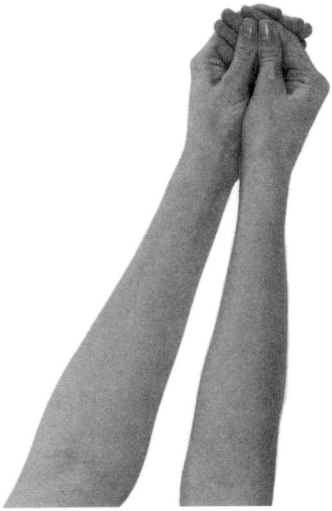

Figure 8.42 Hand position for forearm pass.

Figure 8.43 Platform tilt.

Error Detection and Correction for Forearm Passing

ERROR A player misjudges, contacting the ball with either the hands or even the upper arms, instead of the forearms.

CORRECTION Watch carefully as the player contacts the ball. Emphasize moving the feet first to get into a balanced position before contacting the ball. The ball should contact the player above the wrist and below the elbow. A player can overcome misjudging the ball by tilting the forearm platform to deflect the ball toward the target. Have the player establish a low position and extend the arms away from the body when contacting the ball. Check the player at contact with the ball. A player's swinging the arms will cause the ball to rebound over the net or away from the target.

ERROR A player's arms are too high when she contacts the ball. Her arms follow through above shoulder height.

CORRECTION Instruct the player to let the ball drop to waist level before contact. She should try to stop her arms on contact by using a "poking" action on the ball.

Forearm Passing Games

LOW PLACES

Goal

To pass effectively to the setter.

Description

The game is played 3 v 3 (see figure 8.44). The objective is to use a forearm pass or dig to receive the serve and put it into playing position for a teammate. Award three points each time a team receives the serve and passes the ball to the middle front position. Teams can receive additional points by completing the play over the net—one point for a two-touch play and two for a three-touch play. However, do not award any points if they don't receive the ball and pass it to the front middle position. Award one point to the team that wins the rally. Alternate serves no matter who wins the rally, and give each team an equal number of serves. Rotate players after each rally.

To make the game easier:

- Allow servers to start closer to the net (some 8- and 9-year-olds won't be able to serve over the net).
- Award one point for receiving the serve and passing to any position, and award three points for receiving the serve and passing the ball to the middle front position.
- Have the coach serve an easy ball directly to the receiver.
- Play 3 v 4 and rotate a player to the receiving side.

To make the game harder:

- Award points only after three consecutive serves have been received and passed to the front middle position.
- Award points only if the ball is called by the receiver and passed appropriately.

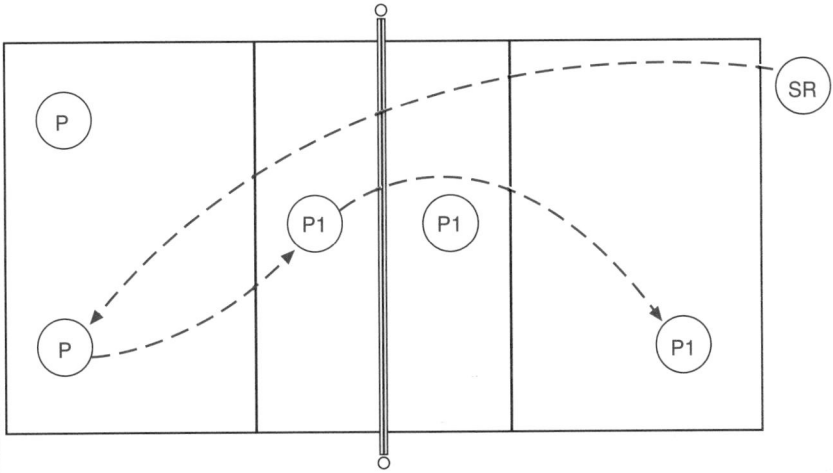

Figure 8.44 Low Places.

CRAZY PASSES

Goal

To forearm pass effectively.

Description

The game is played 4 v 4 (see figure 8.45). A player begins the game with an overhand or underhand serve, then a passer uses a forearm pass to get the ball to a designated setter. The setter passes the ball to the next passer, who forearm passes the ball back to the setter. The setter then passes the ball to a third passer, who again forearm passes the ball back. When three players complete forearm passes, award the team two points. Once the three players have attempted forearm passes, the team is allowed to overhead pass or hit the ball to the other side of the net. Alternate serves between teams, regardless of who wins the rally, and give each team an equal number of serves. Rotate players after each rally.

To make the game easier:

- Allow teams five attempts to make three successful passes to the setter.

To make the game harder:

- Play 3 v 3.

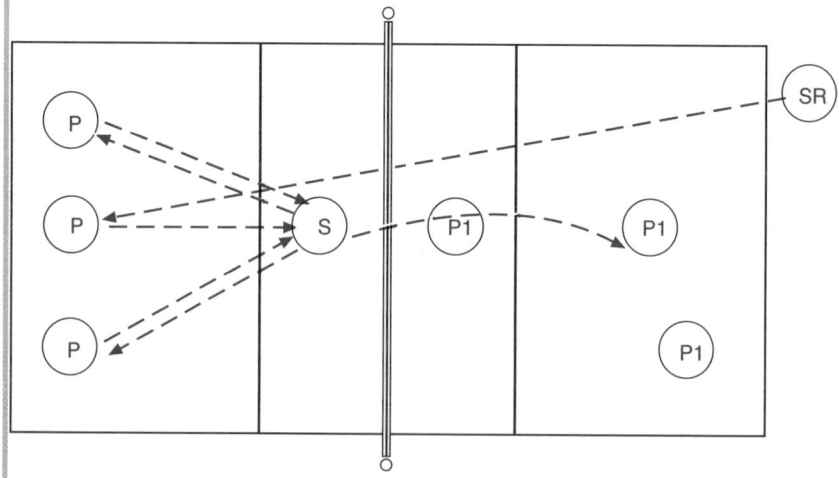

Figure 8.45 Crazy Passes.

- Define a "successful pass" as one that can be set by the setter. Award a point only when the ball is successfully passed three consecutive times to the setter.

TARGET PASSING

Goal

To set up the attack through forearm passing.

Description

The game is played 3 v 3 (see figure 8.46). The objective is to use a forehand pass to pass to a player in front of the net, who can then set the ball up for a hit. Award points for forehand passes that go into a marked square (an area five feet by five feet) in front of the net and can be set by another player. Play is continuous until a sideout occurs. Keep score for each team. Alternate serves between teams, regardless of who wins the rally, and give each team an equal number of serves. Rotate players after each rally.

To make the game easier:

- Players only have to get the ball in the target area, not to the setter, to get points.
- Play 4 v 4.

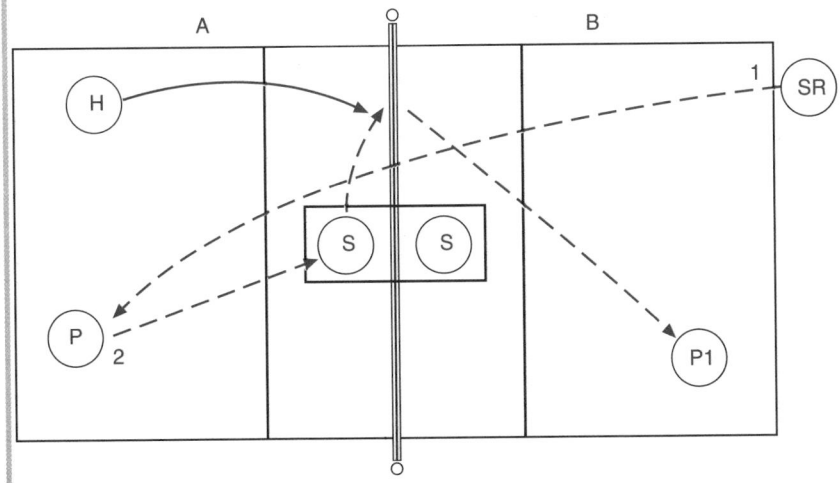

Figure 8.46 Target Passing.

(continued)

Target Passing *(continued)*

To make the game harder:

- Play 2 v 2.
- Decrease the size of the target area to three feet by three feet.
- Move the target area to either side.

PASSING CAN

Goal

To improve forearm passing accuracy.

Description

The game is played with one server and three players (see figure 8.47). The objective is to use a forehand pass to pass the ball into one of three garbage cans in front of the net. If players do not arc the ball, the ball will not fall into a can. Award the team two points every time a ball goes into a can (even if it bounces out). Serve five balls for each team, and add up the points when all the balls have been served.

To make the game easier:

- Have players toss the ball instead of serving.

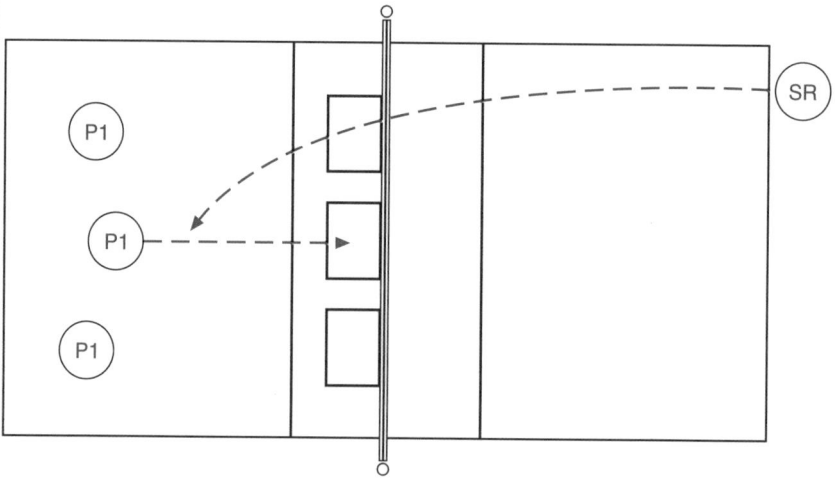

Figure 8.47 Passing Can.

- Allow two touches.
- Move the back line closer to the target cans.

To make the game harder:

- Have only one or two garbage cans.

Serving

Besides putting the ball in play, the serve can be an effective way for a team to score points quickly. A good server can provide the momentum to boost his team to victory. The server may choose to serve underhand, roundhouse, or overhand. In youth volleyball, the server usually learns the underhand serve first. In this section we'll cover five serves: the free-ball toss serve, the underhand serve, the roundhouse serve, the overhand serve, and the jump serve.

Free-Ball Toss Serve

A free-ball toss serve is the easiest way for youngsters to put the ball in play. The server simply tosses the ball over the net using an overhand throwing motion to do so. We recommend using this serve for 8- and 9-year-olds, at least early in the season.

Underhand Serve

The underhand serve allows beginning players to put the ball in play. It is easier to control than the overhand serve because it doesn't involve a toss. Here are some coaching points you should make as you introduce the skill:

1. Start with the weight on the back foot and the ball held in front of the toe by the "shelf" (nonhitting) hand.
2. Keep the eyes focused on the ball until contact is made with the heel of the hand. Transfer weight from the back to the front foot as the arm swings to contact the ball (see figure 8.48a).
3. Drop the shelf hand and immediately hit the ball.
4. Follow through with the hitting arm toward the top of the net. The hitting arm and back leg should be in line with the follow-through (see figure 8.48b).

Figure 8.48 Proper technique for the underhand serve.

Error Detection and Correction for Underhand Serving

ERROR The ball goes up more than forward and does not travel over the net.

CORRECTION Tell the player to hold the ball at waist level or lower, contact the ball just below center back, and swing her arm forward toward the net. As she does, she should transfer her weight to their forward foot.

ERROR The ball does not have enough force to make it over the net.

CORRECTION The player should not swing her holding hand; she should hit a stationary ball, making contact with the heel of their open hand.

ERROR Following her serves, the player stands behind the serving line and watches her serves.

CORRECTION On all serves (including roundhouse, overhand, and jump serves), the player should move forward into the court and assume a defensive position.

Roundhouse Serve

A player can generate more power with the roundhouse serve than she can with an underhand serve because the roundhouse calls on larger muscle groups. However, it does take more skill because it requires a toss, which should be in front of the nonhitting shoulder to allow the player time to swing her arm and contact the ball at full extension. The toss should be made with little or no spin. Instruct the player to perform the roundhouse serve as follows:

1. Stand facing the sideline with your forward foot toward a net post (see figure 8.49a).
2. Toss the ball slightly ahead of your body, away from the midline, and toward your nonhitting shoulder.
3. Fully extend your arm throughout the entire motion of the serve. Drop your arm back and then swing it up over your head, making contact with the ball directly in front of your body.
4. As you swing your arm, shift your weight forward onto your front foot, rotate your hips forward, and immediately follow with your shoulder, bringing your hitting arm into contact with the ball (see figure 8.49b).

5. Contact the ball with an open hand just below the center back of the ball—a poking action with no wrist snap and little follow-through (see figure 8.49c).
6. Turn your body and move toward the court.

Figure 8.49 Proper technique for the roundhouse serve.

Error Detection and Correction for Roundhouse Serving

ERROR The ball goes into the net.

CORRECTION The toss is too far ahead of the player's nonhitting shoulder or too low.

ERROR The serve does not reach the net.

CORRECTION The server should rotate her body into the contact, hitting the ball with the heel of an open hand.

Overhand Serve

The overhand serve is also more challenging for novice players than underhand serving because it requires being able to toss consistently. The overhand serve requires more coordination, timing, and strength, so teach it to players only after they have mastered the underhand serve. Many young players will doubt their ability to serve over the net with the overhand serve. A general test to see if they are indeed capable of serving over the net is to check if they can throw the ball over the net from the serving area. If they can throw over the net, most likely they can also serve overhand. The overhand serve, when mastered, is more versatile as it allows for greater speed, power, and control than the underhand serve.

The toss is the key to a successful overhand serve. A ball tossed too high, too low, too far in front, or too far in back will cause the server to

Error Detection and Correction for Overhand Serving

ERROR The toss is inconsistent, which makes for an unreliable and uncontrolled serve.

CORRECTION Check that the shelf hand is tossing the ball in front of the hitting shoulder. Have the player practice tossing without hitting the ball—to help him concentrate on tossing to the correct height (for the overhand serve, 12 to 18 inches from the shelf hand with the arm extended). Make sure the server's feet are properly positioned. The server should be making contact with the heel of the hand at the one o'clock position. Remind the server to swing his hitting arm as fast as he can.

"chase" the toss and move out of proper precontact alignment. A server should think of the ball as an extension of the shelf hand reaching up. Tell the player to "lift" the ball above the shelf hand when that arm is fully extended. The toss should always be in front of the hitting shoulder (see figure 8.50). Let the player practice the whole skill of serving—but have her focus on the toss until it becomes consistent on each

Figure 8.50 Overhand serve toss.

repetition. Here are some coaching points you should make as you instruct players in this skill:

1. Stand with a slight stride position, shoulders square to the net, foot of the noncontact side forward, weight evenly distributed (see figure 8.51a).
2. As you toss the ball, bring your hitting arm back with the elbow high and hand close to your ear.
3. Swing your arm forward keeping your eyes on the ball (see figure 8.51b).
4. Contact the center back of the ball with the heel of your open hand.

(continued)

Figure 8.51 Proper technique for the overhand serve.

c

Figure 8.51 *(continued)*

5. Use a poking action with little or no follow-through; transfer your weight to your front foot (see figure 8.51c).
6. Continue forward to assume a defensive position.

Jump Serve

The jump serve is the most difficult of the five serves to master because it involves not only proper technique (as in the overhand serve) but also accurate timing in the jump. The jump serve can add power to the serve and make it more difficult for opponents to handle. Players love to jump serve and should be encouraged to learn it. It will improve their overhand serves and spiking skills.

The toss is crucial in executing a good jump serve. A ball tossed too high, too low, or too far in front will cause the server to "chase" the toss and move out of proper precontact alignment. Servers should think of the ball as an extension of the shelf hand reaching up. Tell players to "lift" the ball above the shelf hand when that arm is fully extended.

The toss should always be in front of the hitting shoulder. It is most common for a player to take a couple of steps toward the endline as she tosses the ball in preparation for jumping. So the toss must be farther out in front of the player than if the player were standing still to serve. It's OK for the server to land in the court as long as she jumps from behind the endline and contacts the ball before landing.

Let players practice the whole skill of serving—but have them focus on the toss until it becomes consistent with each repetition. Here are some coaching points you should make as you instruct players in this skill:

1. Stand with a slight stride position, shoulders square to the net, foot of the noncontact side forward, weight on the back foot (see figure 8.52a).

a b c

Figure 8.52 Proper technique for the jump serve.

2. Initiate the serve by stepping forward with the front foot. Take a regular three-step approach, as with a spike, and toss the ball after completing the first step. The toss will need to be farther in front of your body than it is when serving from a stationary position.
3. As you toss the ball, bring your hitting arm back with the elbow high and hand close to your ear (see figure 8.52b).
4. Swing your arm forward keeping your eyes on the ball.
5. Contact the center back of the ball with your open hand (see figure 8.52c).
6. Snap your wrist and follow through as with a spike.
7. Continue forward to assume a defensive position.

Serving Game

SERVICE FOR FOUR

Goal

To hit serves accurately.

Description

The game is played 2 v 2 (see figure 8.53). The objective is to hit the ball into one of four quadrants using either an underhand or overhand serve, so divide the court into four quadrants using tape. Award

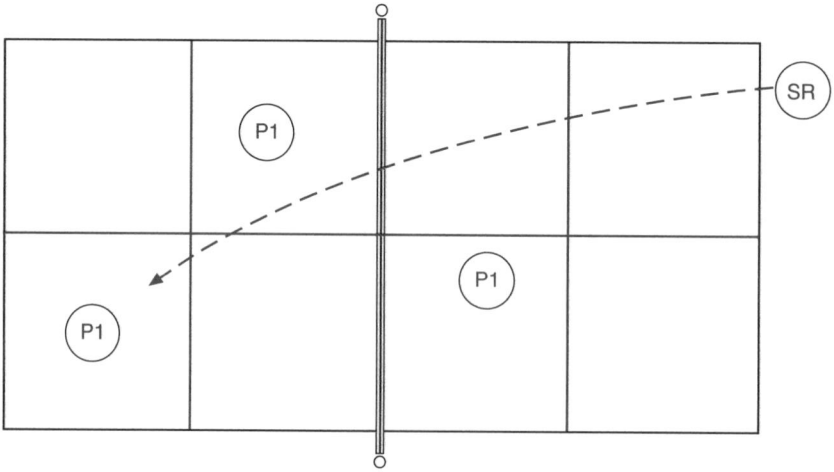

Figure 8.53 Service for Four.

five points for calling the serve; award two points for serving into one of the two back quadrants; and award one point for serving into one of the two front quadrants. If the player serves to a quadrant, award points even if the ball is returned. Keep score for each server, and continue play until one player reaches 25 points. Players should try to return service and volley the ball. Let each server get three serves before alternating serves. Have players rotate positions when the serve alternates.

To make the game easier:

- Award points for any service over the net (even if it goes out).
- Lower the net.

To make the game harder:

- Award points only if the player can call the quadrant.
- Award points only if the ball touches the ground in the quadrant called.
- Reduce the size of the court or increase the number of target areas.

Serve-Receiving

The reception of serve is the starting point of your team's attempt to win the point under the rally scoring system. A successful serve reception allows your team to begin your attack and win the rally. To successfully receive the serve, players must be able to anticipate the direction of the ball and determine who will receive it. The sooner it is determined who will receive the serve, the more time that player has to get into the correct position.

The best means of predicting the direction of the opponent's serve is to concentrate on the server's body. Players should look for the angle of the server's shoulders, the direction the forward foot is pointing, and the direction of the hitting arm (see figure 8.54). Players should call for the ball by yelling, "Mine!" This call should be made before the ball crosses the net. The player calling for the ball must quickly move to the correct location to receive the serve, set his position, and execute the forearm pass to initiate the attack (see figure 8.55).

Digging

The performance of the dig is somewhat similar to that of the forearm pass. The main difference is that in the forearm pass, a player has time

Figure 8.54 The server's body position is the best means for predicting the direction of the serve.

Figure 8.55 The serve-receiver should execute the forearm pass to initiate the attack.

to move, set her position, and play the ball. In the dig, however, she must react and play the ball with little time to strategically position herself. When digging a ball, the player should allow it to drop as low as possible, increasing the time she has to play it. She should cushion the ball, absorbing the force from a hard-driven spike, and direct it high and toward the general vicinity of the center of the court, making it easier for the setter to play it (see figure 8.56). She should flick her wrists or flex her elbows at contact to gain height and to ensure that the ball will remain on her side of the net.

Figure 8.56 Proper technique for a dig.

Error Detection and Correction for Digging

ERROR The ball goes straight up or back over the player's head.

CORRECTION Stop the arms on contact by using a "poking" action on the ball. Let the ball drop to waist level or lower before contact.

ERROR The ball is low and fast as it leaves the digger's arms.

CORRECTION The digger should bend her knees, keeping her back straight, as she moves under the ball. She should also touch the floor with her hands to stay in a low position.

ERROR The ball does not go high (two or three feet above the net) and toward the center of the court.

CORRECTION The digger should flick her wrists or flex her elbows on contact.

Digging Game

DOWN AND UP

Goal

To dig the ball effectively.

Description

The game is played 2 v 2 (see figure 8.57). Place a starting line 1 meter from the service line, and suspend a target rope parallel to the net (6 to 10 feet in the air) on each side of the net. (If you don't have a place to suspend the ropes, have four people hold the ropes up.) Have the players on the team receiving the ball start behind the starting line. Team A initiates play by tossing the ball to team B so that team B players have to dig the ball. The dig must send the ball over the rope on team B's side of the court for the team to win a point. Players should try to hit the ball in front of the starting line (if the ball goes past the starting line, it is out). Players must stay behind the starting line until the ball has been hit so that they are forced to dig the ball. Alternate serves between teams, regardless of who wins the rally, and give each team an equal number of serves. Rotate players after each rally.

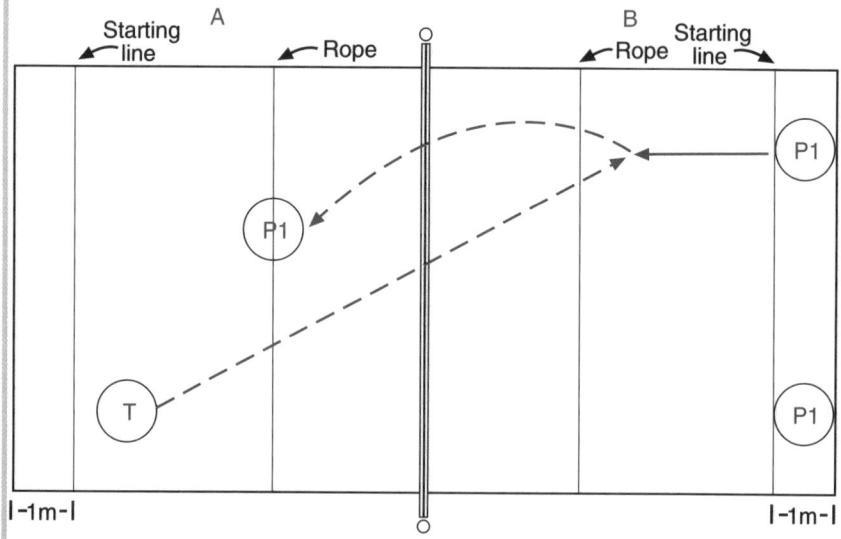

Figure 8.57 Down and Up.

To make the game easier or more continuous:

- Lower the target rope.
- Increase the number of players.

To make the game harder:

- Move the starting line farther back.
- Continue normal play after the "dig point" and allow regular point scoring as well.

Blocking

A good block involves ability in timing and in reading the offensive hitter's intentions. As you introduce blocking to your team, emphasize that every member, short or tall, can play an effective role as a blocker. Although taller players have an advantage, shorter players can also block to deflect and slow down hard-driven spikes.

The objective in blocking is to block a hard-driven spike back into the opponent's court or to deflect it high into the air on the blocker's side of the court. Without the block, an offensive team's spike very likely will earn a point. In youth volleyball with a smaller court and fewer players, blocking is limited to one blocker and some simple footwork.

Ready Position for Blocking

The ready position gets your players aligned to set a good block. Begin by teaching your players to stand facing the net with their hands held shoulder-width apart at head level. The hands should be open with the fingers spread and the palms facing the net. The knees are slightly bent, and the weight is on the balls of the feet. Players will move in this coiled position, ready to spring up to block an opponent's attack (see figure 8.58).

Hand Position for Blocking

As the blocker jumps to block, the hands should surround and smother the ball (see figure 8.59). The blocker's fingers are spread and angled to deflect the ball toward the floor. The hands do not wave or flail at the ball. A blocker who is short, a weak jumper, or late jumping to block may perform a soft block (see figure 8.60). The blocker's fingers are still spread, but the hands are angled backward toward the blocker's court. The soft block merely deflects the ball back into the blocker's court to be played by teammates. The rules allow the blocker's team to make three more contacts if a soft block is deflected and playable.

Figure 8.58 Ready position for a block.

Figure 8.59 Hand position for a block.

Figure 8.60 Hand position for a soft block.

Footwork for Blocking

A blocker moving along the net uses a step-close-step footwork pattern to get into position across from the hitter. From the semicrouched, ready position for blocking (see figure 8.61a), the player steps first with the leg closer to the direction in which she intends to move (see figure 8.61b). Next, the blocker closes the feet together by pushing off the trailing foot. The feet do not cross. The player is now ready to explode up to block the attack (see figure 8.61c). In most cases, the blocker should jump after the attacker, since the attacker must swing at the ball after jumping. This step-close-step footwork helps the player control momentum and maintain balance as she blocks. Remind players to stay away from the net and off the centerline. They should land on both feet and be ready to move in any direction after blocking.

Figure 8.61 Proper technique for blocking.

Error Detection and Correction for Blocking

ERROR Hard-driven and off-speed attacks are deflecting off the blocker and going out of bounds.

CORRECTION The blocker must keep his body parallel to the net, with the hands extended above the net if possible, facing the court. The blocker should turn the outside hand in toward the court so that the ball will rebound back into the attacker's court. The blocker should keep the hands firm and strong, angled for a deflection to rebound directly down (unless the blocker is executing a soft block). The blocker should jump after the attacker has jumped, which gives a greater chance for the ball to be blocked.

Blocking Game

BLOCK-OUT

Goal

To block hits effectively.

Description

The game is played 4 v 4 (see figure 8.62). Team A serves to team B and then sets up with three people in front of the net for a one- or two-player block. Play out the rally and award points for blocks. Award three points for blocks that remain inbounds on the attackers' side of the court; award two points if the block prevents the ball from entering the defenders' court. Play is continuous; have someone keep score from the sideline (parent, manager, injured player). Alternate serves between teams, no matter who wins the rally, and give each team an equal number of serves. Rotate players after each rally. The first team to 20 is the winner.

To make the game easier:

- Play 5 v 5 or 6 v 6.
- Lower the net.

To make the game harder:

- Play 3 v 3.
- Award points only for blocks that remain inbounds and are on the other side of the net.

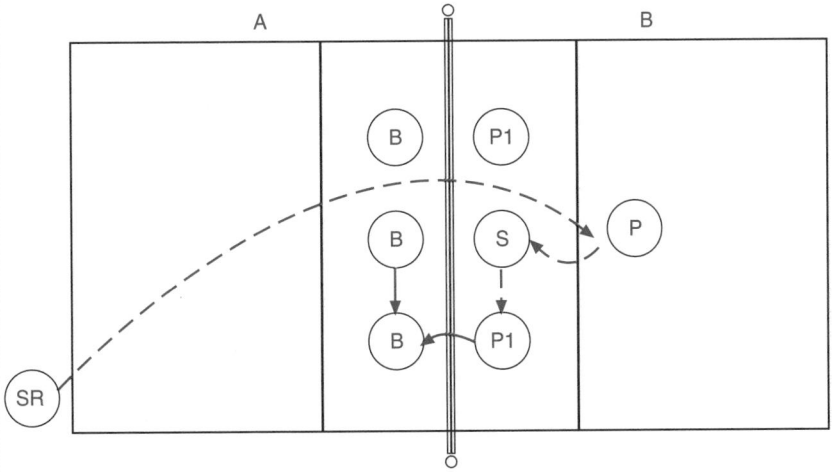

Figure 8.62 Block-Out.

Pursuing and Saving

The pursuing and saving of an errant pass is one of the more dramatic plays in volleyball. Because a ball is not out of bounds until it lands or strikes an object out of bounds, players can range far off the court to track down a ball and pass it to the center of their court so that it can be returned, keeping it in play.

The player should pursue a ball with her hands apart because running with her hands in passing position will slow her pursuit. As she nears the errant pass, she should get her arms in passing position, keeping a platform parallel to the ground, and hit a high, playable ball toward the center of the court. The pass she uses is called a reverse forearm pass, in which the ball is hit directly over her head back toward the center of the court (see figure 8.63). She should keep her back to the court, rather than trying to twist or turn back to the court as she reaches the ball. As an athlete is pursuing the ball, teammates should shift into position to support the expected pass, preparing for the best possible hit.

Figure 8.63 Reverse forearm pass.

chapter 9

Season Plans

Hopefully you've learned a lot from this book: what your responsibilities as a coach are, how to communicate well and provide for safety, how to use the games approach to teach and shape skills, and how to coach on game days. But game days make up only a portion of your season—you and your players will spend more time in practice than in competition. How well you conduct practices and prepare your players for competition will greatly affect both your and your players' enjoyment and success throughout the season.

In this chapter, then, we present three season plans: one for 8- to 9-year-olds, one for 10- to 11-year-olds, and one for 12- to 14-year-olds. Use these plans as guidelines for conducting your practices. These plans are not the *only* way to approach your season, but they do present an appropriate teaching progression. Remember to incorporate the games approach as you use these plans, using Game 1 to put your players in a game-like situation that introduces them to the main tactic or skill that you want them to learn that day. Then guide your players through a short question-and-answer session that leads to the skill practice. Here you should conduct one or two skill practices in which you will teach players the tactic or skill and then conduct a fun drill for them to practice that skill.

Refer to chapter 5 (page 48) for how to run a practice. In chapter 8 you will find descriptions of all the tactics and skills, and games you can use to practice them. Throughout the season plans we refer you to the appropriate pages for those tactics and skills and games.

Remember to keep the introductions, demonstrations, and explanations of the tactics and skills brief. As the players practice, attend to individual players, guiding them with tips or with further demonstration.

Good luck and good coaching!

Season Plan for 8- to 9-year-olds

Many 8- to 9-year-olds have had little or no exposure to volleyball. Don't assume they have any knowledge of the game. Help them explore the basic tactics and skills of the sport as suggested in the following season plan.

Practice 1

- **Purpose:** Introduction to the game and the team
- **Warm-up**
- **Game:** Overhead passing game (Game 7: Setting Pretty, pp. 120)
- **Skill Development of overhead passing**
- **Game:** (Game 7: Setting Pretty, pp. 120)
- **Cool-down and Review**

Practice 2

- **Purpose:** Introduction to the game
- **Warm-up**
- **Game:** Overhead passing game (Game 8: Pass to Paradise, pp. 121)
- **Skill Development of overhead passing**
- **Game:** Overhead passing game (Game 8: Pass to Paradise, pp. 121)
- **Cool-down and Review**

Practice 3

- **Purpose:** Forearm passing
- **Warm-up**

- **Game:** Forearm passing game (Game 1: Low Places, pp. 124)
- **Skill Development of forearm passing**
- **Game:** Forearm passing game (Game 1: Low Places, pp. 124)
- **Cool-down and Review**

Practice 4

- **Purpose:** Forearm passing
- **Warm-up**
- **Game:** Forearm passing game (Game 12: Passing Can, pp. 128)
- **Introduce receiving serve game**
- **Game:** Receiving serve game (Game 5: Crazy Passes, pp. 128)
- **Cool-down and Review**

Practice 5

- **Purpose:** Serving
- **Warm-up**
- **Game:** Serving game (Game 6: Service for Four, pp. 138)
- **Skill Development for serving**
- **Game:** Serving game (Game 6: Service for Four, pp. 138)
- **Cool-down and Review**

Practice 6

- **Purpose:** Serving
- **Warm-up**
- **Game:** Serving game (Game 6: Service for Four, pp. 138)
- **Review serving, receiving, and passing**
- **Game:** Combination play (Game 2: Three Hits, pp. 88)
- **Cool-down and Review**

Practice 7

- **Purpose:** Receiving off the serve (underhand)
- **Warm-up**
- **Game:** Receiving game (Game 9: Target Passing, pp. 127)
- **Skill Review for serving**
- **Game:** Receiving game (Game 9: Target Passing, pp. 127)
- **Cool-down and Review**

Practice 8

- **Purpose:** Forearm passing
- **Warm-up**
- **Game:** Forearm passing game (Game 5: Crazy Passes, pp. 126)
- **Skill Review for forearm passing**
- **Game:** Forearm passing game (Game 5: Crazy Passes, pp. 126)
- **Cool-down and Review**

Practice 9

- **Purpose:** Overhead passing (Setting)
- **Warm-up**
- **Game:** Overhead passing game (Game 7: Setting Pretty, pp. 120)
- **Skill Review for passing**
- **Game:** Combination play game (Game 2: Three Hits, pp. 88)
- **Cool-down and Review**

Practice 10

- **Purpose:** Positions
- **Warm-up**
- **Game:** Forearm and overhead passing game (Game 5: Crazy Passes, pp. 126)
- **Skill Review for passing**
- **Game:** Combination play game (Game 2: Three Hits, pp. 88)
- **Cool-down and Review**

Practice 11

- **Purpose:** Serving
- **Warm-up**
- **Game:** Service game (Game 6: Service for Four, pp. 138)
- **Skill Review for serving**
- **Scrimmage with focus on service placement**
- **Cool-down and Review**

Practice 12

- **Purpose:** Combination play / positions
- **Warm-up**

- **Game:** Combination game (Game 2: Three Hits, pp. 88)
- **Skill Review for playing**
- **Scrimmage**
- **Cool-down and Review**

Practice 13

- **Purpose:** Combination play / positions
- **Warm-up**
- **Game:** Combination game (Game 2: Three Hits, pp. 88)
- **Skill Review for playing**
- **3 v 3 tournament**
- **Cool-down and Review**

Practice 14

- **Purpose:** Combination play / positions
- **Warm-up**
- **Game:** Combination game (Game 2: Three Hits, pp. 88)
- **Skill Review for playing**
- **Scrimmage**
- **Cool-down and Review**

Season Plan for 10- to 11-year-olds

This season plan builds upon the previous one as players practice the fundamental tactics and skills and add a few new tactics, including positioning, hitting the ball, and executing the dig.

Practice 1

- **Purpose:** Introduction to the team
- **Warm-up**
- **Game:** Overhead passing game (Game 8: Pass to Paradise, pp. 121)
- **Skill Development of overhead passing**
- **Game:** Overhead passing game (Game 8: Pass to Paradise, pp. 121)
- **Cool-down and Review**

Practice 2

- **Purpose:** Introduction to forearm passing
- **Warm-up**
- **Game:** Forearm passing game (Game 12: Passing Can, pp. 128)
- **Skill Development of forearm passing**
- **Game:** Forearm passing game (Game 12: Passing Can, pp. 128)
- **Cool-down and Review**

Practice 3

- **Purpose:** Serving (Underhand)
- **Warm-up**
- **Game:** Serving game (Game 6: Service for Four, pp. 138)
- **Skill Development of serving**
- **Game:** Serving game (Game 6: Service for Four, pp. 138)
- **Cool-down and Review**

Practice 4

- **Purpose:** Receiving serve
- **Warm-up**
- **Game:** Forearm passing game (Game 1: Low Places, pp. 124)
- **Introduce receiving serve game**
- **Game:** Forearm passing game (Game 1: Low Places, pp. 124)
- **Cool-down and Review**

Practice 5

- **Purpose:** Combination play
- **Warm-up**
- **Game:** Combination play game (Game 2: Three Hits, pp. 88)
- **Tactical Development**
- **Game:** Combination play game (Game 2: Three Hits, pp. 88)
- **Cool-down and Review**

Practice 6

- **Purpose:** Positioning
- **Warm-up**

- **Game:** Serving game (Game 10: Skeet Shooting, pp. 115)
- **Review serving, receiving, and passing**
- **Game:** Combination play (Game 9: Target Passing, pp. 127)
- **Cool-down and Review**

Practice 7

- **Purpose:** Hitting the ball
- **Warm-up**
- **Game:** Hitting game (Game 4: Hammer Time, pp. 114)
- **Skill Development for hitting**
- **Game:** Hitting game (Game 4: Hammer Time, pp. 114)
- **Cool-down and Review**

Practice 8

- **Purpose:** Hitting the ball
- **Warm-up**
- **Game:** Hitting game (Game 4: Hammer Time, pp. 114)
- **Skill Review for hitting**
- **Game:** Combination play (Game 9: Target Passing, pp. 127)
- **Cool-down and Review**

Practice 9

- **Purpose:** Overhead passing (Setting)
- **Warm-up**
- **Game:** Overhead passing game (Game 8: Pass to Paradise, pp. 121)
- **Skill Review for passing**
- **Game:** Combination play (Game 9: Target Passing, pp. 127)
- **Cool-down and Review**

Practice 10

- **Purpose:** The dig
- **Warm-up**
- **Game:** Dig game (Game 11: Down and Up, pp. 142)
- **Skill Development for Digging**
- **Game:** Dig game (Game 11: Down and Up, pp. 142)
- **Cool-down and Review**

Practice 11

- **Purpose:** Serving (Overhand Serve)
- **Warm-up**
- **Game:** Service game (Game 10: Skeet Shooting, pp. 115)
- **Skill Development for serving**
- **Game:** Service game (Game 10: Skeet Shooting, pp. 115)
- **Cool-down and Review**

Practice 12

- **Purpose:** Serving (overhand serve)
- **Warm-up**
- **Game:** Service game (Game 10: Skeet Shooting, pp. 115)
- **Skill Review for serving**
- **Scrimmage**
- **Cool-down and Review**

Practice 13

- **Purpose:** Combination play / positions
- **Warm-up**
- **Game:** Combination game (Game 2: Three Hits, pp. 88)
- **Skill Review for playing**
- **3 v 3 tournament**
- **Cool-down and Review**

Practice 14

- **Purpose:** Combination play / positions
- **Warm-up**
- **Game:** Combination game (Game 2: Three Hits, pp. 88)
- **Skill Review for playing**
- **Scrimmage**
- **Cool-down and Review**

Season Plan for12- to14-year-olds

At this stage players are refining the skills they have learned from past years. This season plan builds upon the previous one and adds a few new skills, including blocking and overhand serves.

Practice 1

- **Purpose:** Introduction to the team
- **Warm-up**
- **Game:** Overhead passing game (Game 8: Pass to Paradise, pp. 121)
- **Skill Review of passing**
- **Game:** Forearm passing game (Game 9: Target Passing, pp. 127)
- **Cool-down and Review**

Practice 2

- **Purpose:** Introduction to hitting
- **Warm-up**
- **Game:** Hitting game (Game 4: Hammer Time, pp. 114)
- **Skill Development of hitting**
- **Game:** Hitting game (Game 4: Hammer Time, pp. 114)
- **Cool-down and Review**

Practice 3

- **Purpose:** Serving (overhand)
- **Warm-up**
- **Game:** Serving game (Game 10: Skeet Shooting, pp. 115)
- **Skill Development of serving**
- **Game:** Serving game (Game 10: Skeet Shooting, pp. 115)
- **Cool-down and Review**

Practice 4

- **Purpose:** Receiving serve
- **Warm-up**
- **Game:** Receiving serve game (Game 1: Low Places, pp. 124)
- **Introduce receiving serve game**
- **Game:** Receiving serve game (Game 1: Low Places, pp. 124)
- **Cool-down and Review**

Practice 5

- **Purpose:** Hitting the ball
- **Warm-up**
- **Game:** Hitting game (Game 4: Hammer Time, pp. 114)
- **Review of hitting skills**
- **Game:** Hitting game (Game 4: Hammer Time, pp. 114)
- **Cool-down and Review**

Practice 6

- **Purpose:** Blocking
- **Warm-up**
- **Game:** Blocking game (Game 3: Blockout, pp. 146)
- **Introduce blocking skill**
- **Game:** Blocking game (Game 3: Blockout, pp. 146)
- **Cool-down and Review**

Practice 7

- **Purpose:** Combination play
- **Warm-up**
- **Game:** Combination play game (Game 2: Three Hits, pp. 88)
- **Review combination strategy**
- **Game:** Combination play game (Game 2: Three Hits, pp. 88)
- **Cool-down and Review**

Practice 8

- **Purpose:** Positioning
- **Warm-up**
- **Game:** Serving game (Game 6: Service for Four, pp. 138)
- **Review position**
- **Game:** Combination play game (Game 2: Three Hits, pp. 88)
- **Cool-down and Review**

Practice 9

- **Purpose:** The dig
- **Warm-up**
- **Game:** Dig game (Game 11: Down and Up, pp. 142)

- **Skill Review for digging**
- **Game:** Dig game (Game 11: Down and Up, pp. 142)
- **Cool-down and Review**

Practice 10

- **Purpose:** The dig
- **Warm-up**
- **Game:** Dig game (Game 11: Down and Up, pp. 142)
- **Skill Development for digging**
- **Game:** Hitting game with focus on digging (Game 4: Hammer Time, pp. 114)
- **Cool-down and Review**

Practice 11

- **Purpose:** Serving (Overhand Serve)
- **Warm-up**
- **Game:** Service game (Game 6: Service for Four, pp. 138)
- **Skill Review for serving**
- **Game:** Service game (Game 6: Service for Four, pp. 138)
- **Cool-down and Review**

Practice 12

- **Purpose:** Serving (overhand serve)
- **Warm-up**
- **Game:** Service game (Game 6: Service for Four, pp. 138)
- **Skill Review for serving**
- **Scrimmage**
- **Cool-down and Review**

Practice 13

- **Purpose:** Combination play / positions
- **Warm-up**
- **Game:** Combination game (Game 2: Three Hits, pp. 88)
- **Skill Review for playing**
- **3 v 3 tournament**
- **Cool-down and Review**

Practice 14

- **Purpose:** Combination play / positions
- **Warm-up**
- **Game:** Combination game (Game 2: Three Hits, pp. 88)
- **Skill Review for playing**
- **Scrimmage**
- **Cool-down and Review**

Injury Report

Name of athlete _____

Date _____

Time _____

First aider (name) _____

Cause of injury _____

_____

Type of injury _____

Anatomical area involved _____

Extent of injury _____

_____

_____

First aid administered _____

_____

_____

Other treatment administered _____

_____

_____

_____

Referral action _____

_____

_____

_____

_____

First aider (signature)

Emergency Information Card

Athlete's name _____ Age _____

Address _____

Phone _____ S.S.# _____

Sport _____

List two persons to contact in case of emergency:

Parent or guardian's name _____

Address _____

Home phone _____ Work phone _____

Second person's name _____

Address _____

Home phone _____ Work phone _____

Relationship to athlete _____

Insurance co. _____ Policy # _____

Physician's name _____ Phone _____

IMPORTANT

Is your child allergic to any drugs? _____ If so, what? _____

Does your child have any other allergies? (e.g., bee stings, dust) _____

Does your child have ____ asthma, ____ diabetes, or ____ epilepsy?

Is your child on any medication? _____ If so, what? _____

Does your child wear contacts? _____

Is there anything else we should know about your child's health or physical condition? If yes, please explain. _____

_____

_____

_____

_____

_____ _____

Signature Date

Emergency Response Card

Information for emergency call
(Be prepared to give this information to the EMS dispatcher.)

1. Location _____

   Street address _____

   City or town _____

   Directions (cross streets, landmarks, etc.) _____

   _____

   _____

2. Telephone number from which call is being made _____
3. Caller's name _____
4. What happened _____

   _____

   _____

   _____

   _____

   _____

5. How many persons injured _____
6. Condition of victim(s) _____
7. Help (first aid) being given _____

   _____

   _____

   _____

Note: Do not hang up first. Let the EMS dispatcher hang up first.

Provide excellent instruction for youth volleyball players

Tens of thousands of youth coaches have benefited from the *Coaching Youth Volleyball* book. Now a new companion videotape will help you create an even more successful coaching experience. The *Coaching Youth Volleyball Video* shows you how to teach the most important volleyball techniques and tactics to your young players.

Approx. 30-minute video
ISBN 0-7360-4000-5
(PAL: ISBN 0-7360-4011-0)

To learn more about ASEP, visit

www.asep.com

To place your order, U.S. customers call

TOLL FREE **1-800-747-4457**

Customers outside the U.S. should place orders using the appropriate telephone number/address in the front of this book.

HUMAN KINETICS
The Premier Publisher for Sports & Fitness
P.O. Box 5076 • Champaign, IL 61825-5076 USA
www.humankinetics.com

2335

6/01